SCOUTING
FOR *BANBURY'S* BOYS

A History of the Scout Movement in Banbury and the Villages of North Oxfordshire

Trevor Parry

Published by
Robert Boyd Publications
260 Colwell Drive, Witney
Oxfordshire OX28 5LW

Distributed by
Trevor Parry
Boundary House
1 Sycamore Drive, Banbury
Oxfordshire OX16 9HF
email: trevorparry@dsl.pipex.com

First edition 2008

Copyright © Trevor Parry

ISBN: 978 1 899536 91 7

Printed and bound by Banbury Litho
Unit 1, Vantage Business Park
Wykham Mill, Bloxham Road
Banbury, Oxon OX16 9UX

Contents

Acknowledgements

Many people have helped me in the production of this book. I would therefore like to take this opportunity to say thank you to them and at the same time acknowledge their contribution to it.

My thanks go to members of the "Times Gone By" Group and to Sue, Stephen and Karey and all of the staff at Banbury Museum. To Alan Donaldson and Mike Snelling of the Bloxham Village History Club; To the Scout Association headquarters staff at Gilwell Park, particularly Pat Styles in Research and Archives. To Jason Gibbins, editor of the Banbury Guardian for permission to reproduce extracts from past editions of the newspaper. To Major Shaw McCloghry, archivist of Bloxham Public School. To John Kirby of the Scout Museum at Youlbury Scout Camp Site, Oxford. To Tom Blinkhorn. To all of the staff at Banbury Reference library (particularly Jean Davis formerly of 4th Banbury). To Lord and Lady Saye and Sele of Broughton Castle. To Jeremy Wilton of the "Four Shires" magazine and to my many friends in Scouting and Guiding locally including Cyril Aston (1st Banbury), Ron and Robert Sangster, Brian Tucker, Ron Marchington and Colin Wain (2nd Banbury), Pete Wroe JP, Bill Dodwell, Dave Sims and Pete Watts (1st Bodicote), Arthur Hosband (1st Bloxham), Jackie Tinkham (1st Grimsbury), Albert Humphris MBE (1st Deddington), Dudley Tann (North Banbury), Peter Whitehead, Bob Herbert and Eileen Dean (7th Banbury) and Eileen Shea (5th Banbury). And of course, last but by no means least, to my wife Janet for her constant support and encouragement.

District Commissioners

Listed below are all of the District Commissioners for Banbury and District together with either their known appointment and resignation or retirement dates or the best estimates available.

Francis Fitzgerald; Appointed 12th July 1912, resigned July 1920.

Commander Cathcart De Trafford; Appointed July 1920, resigned 1923.

The Hon Geoffrey Fiennes; (Later the 19th Baron Lord Saye and Sele). Appointed 1928, resigned June 1948 due to ill health.

J R Railton; Appointed June 1948, resigned 1954.

H F Golding; Appointed January 1955, resigned 1963.

Ron Beck; Appointed 1963, resigned 31st March 1965.

Harold Hobbs; Appointed 1st April 1965, resigned 16th April 1969.

Trevor Parry; Appointed 1st May 1969, resigned 14th May 1983.

Ron Marchington; Appointed 1st June 1983, retired 31st December 1991.

Keith Hicks; Appointed 1st January 1992, resigned 31st December 1994.

Bob Scott; Appointed 1st January 1995, resigned 31st March 2000.

Brian Sargent; Appointed 1st April 2000 to date.

Introduction

For the past few years whenever I have met with some of my many scouting friends and particularly some of the older ones we often reminisce about "old times" and the conversation will usually end with the words "Someone should sit down and write the history of Scouting locally before it is to late" and the reply always seems to be "Yes, someone should" but without saying who that someone should be.

I was thinking about this several months ago and I was reminded of a dear old Sunday School teacher at Marlborough Road Methodist Church where as a young boy I used to go to Sunday School. His name was Horace Salmon, on Sundays he was the Sunday School Superintendent and during the weekdays he was, with his brother Arthur, a maker of boiled sweets and humbugs in North Bar Place, Banbury. He used to stand up in front of us most Sundays and "sermonise". Most of what he said either went over my head or in one ear and out of the other except for one particular Sunday when he stood up and pointed his finger at us (me?) and said "Never point the finger because when you do you point three back at yourself. Only point the finger when having tried three times you have failed. Then and only then may you point the finger."

So who was the person at whom we were "pointing the finger" to the write this history? Perhaps as Horace said I should try and if I fail then perhaps I could get someone else to take on the task. So here goes!

What follows is my attempt at writing a history of scouting locally. I am not a writer or an author, nor am I a historian; I am just trying to ensure that what has happened with Scouting in North Oxfordshire and the many adults who have played their part in its progress over the past one hundred years is recorded and acknowledged. Bearing this in mind please forgive any errors and omissions that occur in the text – they are not intentional.

What I have tried to do is base my "history" on the three "Rs". Not the usual educational three Rs, but R for report, R for research and R for Reminisce.

The first part of the book is a brief life story of Baden-Powell up to the publishing of Scouting for Boys, to set the scene and explain how Scouting came into being; the R for report.

The second part from 1908 to 1949 is based on researching archive copies of the Banbury Advertiser and the Banbury Guardian plus any archive material that still exists locally or in the Scout Association archives; the R for research.

And the third part is based on my experiences within the movement locally from January 1948 onwards; the R for reminisce.

I have thoroughly enjoyed working on this book and I hope that you will get pleasure from reading what is, I believe, a fascinating story.

It is the story of exceptional characters who have been involved in scouting locally and it is dedicated to those many, many people who have given of their time and expertise for the benefit of the young people of North Oxfordshire over the past one hundred years. Truly, they are unsung heroes who deserved to be remembered.

This is by nature a short book and little more than a summary of all that has happened. Everyone who has been involved in Scouting in a meaningful fashion will have special memories of their own. I hope that in reading this book you will have been reminded of these magical times and people you may have met as a part of this great movement.

Lord Baden-Powell of Gilwell. Chief Scout of the World.
Portrait by David Jagger 1929.

CHAPTER ONE

Baden-Powell

Robert Stephenson Smyth Baden-Powell (Stephe to his family) was born in 1857 and after a happy but academically mediocre schooling at Charterhouse was commissioned in the 13th Hussars. He served his country on three continents; Europe, India and Africa rising to the rank of Inspector General of Cavalry.

At the age of 19 he was posted to India and it was here that he delivered a series of lectures to his troops on fieldcraft, mapping and tracking. These were published in book form under the title of "Reconnaissance and Scouting". In due course he persuaded his superiors to recognise the skills of the men trained by him by allowing them to wear a badge on their uniform in the form of a fleur-de-lis, which is used to indicate the north point of a compass. This remains the distinctive emblem of scouting world wide to this day.

In 1899, just before he sailed for South Africa, he sent his publisher another book entitled "Aids to Scouting for NCOs and Men" which drew on and expanded upon his earlier book. This was published whilst he was in South Africa.

On arriving in South Africa in July of that year, the Boer War was just beginning and Baden-Powell was appointed to take charge of the military garrison at Mafeking. It has been said that Mafeking was an insignificant outpost of empire and not worth defending. The Boers thought differently and besieged the town. Mafeking had a civilian population of almost 7,000. It was the administrative centre of the Bechuanaland Protectorate and of the north-eastern region of Cape Colony. It was the most important commercial centre for 100 miles around. It had a railway line linking it to Cape Town in the south and Bulawayo in the north, and it also held valuable railway stock and other supplies.

Mafeking was besieged by the Boers from 14th October 1899 until 17th May 1900. Reports of happenings during the siege were smuggled out of town and were reported widely in the British press where they caught the imagination of the people.

During the siege young boys, some as young as nine were used to supplement the garrison's armed forces doing such work as orderlies, messengers and working in the soup kitchens, thus releasing more men to man the defensive trenches and repulse the Boers. This band of young cadets greatly impressed Baden-Powell, particularly how well they responded to responsibility being placed upon them.

Mafeking was relieved on the 19th May 1900 after 214 days under siege.

News of the relief was reported in the British national press and the country went wild, with large crowds thronging the streets in wild celebration. In Banbury a large bonfire was lit in Cow Fair in front of the town hall which melted the tarmac and, it is rumoured, the heat from the fire blistered the front door of Hunt Edmunds, the brewer's offices on the south side of Cow Fair. A new word entered the English language; the verb to maffick. Baden-Powell became a national hero.

CHAPTER TWO

Scouting for Boys

On his return to the UK in 1903 Baden-Powell found that his book "Aids to Scouting for NCOs and Men" was being used by the Boys Brigade (a movement formed some twenty years earlier) and by Public Schools. He also started receiving letters from boys regarding his book seeking advice from their hero. He replied to all of the letters. He therefore determined to rewrite the book for more general use. In 1907, in order to formulate and to put to the test ideas that he had been developing in his own mind

B-P at his experimental Camp on Brownsea Island in Poole Harbour, August 1907.

for some considerable time, he organised an experimental camp for boys which was held in August 1907 on Brownsea Island in Poole Harbour. It was highly successful and encouraged him to develop his ideas further. This was to be the birth of Scouting.

The first of six fortnightly parts of "Scouting for Boys" was published in January 1908 at a cost of 4d (under 2 pence in today's currency). It was a great success; the first complete edition was printed in May 1908 at a cost of 2 shillings (10p) and reprinted a further five times that year and five times again in 1909.

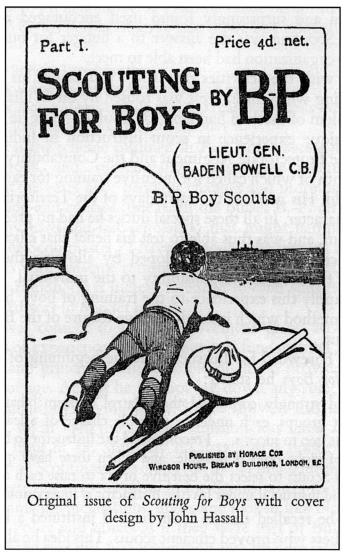

Original issue of *Scouting for Boys* with cover design by John Hassall

Front cover of Part 1 "Scouting for Boys" Published Jan 15, 1908.

"Scouting for Boys" was published by Charles Pearson, a Canadian publishing entrepreneur and a supporter of Baden-Powell and his ideals. In April 1908 in order to maintain interest in the Boy Scout Movement and also for financial gain, Pearson with the approval of Baden-Powell launched a weekly penny magazine called "The Scout" which contained amongst other things stories of adventure and instructional articles. In its first year it reached a circulation of over 100,000 copies per week. It was through "The Scout" that Baden-Powell was able to guide the Movement before any other official ways were available. He also contributed a weekly article to the magazine almost without break for the next thirty years.

The effect of "Scouting for Boys" on the young boys of the day was spectacular. Small groups of lads could be seen around the country putting into practice things that they had read about in "Scouting for Boys" written by their hero, General Baden-Powell; or "B-P" as he became known. They were soon to be found helping old ladies across the street, lighting camp fires in fields and woods and chopping down trees.

Such an unco-ordinated state of affairs could not be allowed to continue unchecked and B-P was soon forced to retire from the army and look after this unorganised mass of young people to bring some order into its management and development. The Scout Association was born.

B-P's major problem was finance; how do you finance a national organisation? In many ways he was naive about money, he had, I understand, refused to accept any royalties from "Scouting for Boys" which has proved to be the fourth largest publication in the world after the Bible, the Koran and the thoughts of Chairman Mao. Fortunately Charles Pearson, the publisher of "Scouting for Boys" and "The Scout" came to his aid. In Pearson's view Scouting was a heaven sent opportunity to make money and so with a degree of what might be termed "enlightened self interest" he provided an office and the staff to man it, and in retrospect he almost hijacked the movement for commercial gain.

The national organisation that B-P set up was set up "on the hoof". He used as his model the only one that he knew; the British Colonial system as practised in India and Africa. This was a very much decentralised structure giving power and authority to those in the field. B-P divided the country into Scout Counties following, in the main, local authority boundaries with a County Commissioner in charge together with an organising committee responsible directly to Scout Headquarters. These

Counties were subdivided into Scout Districts made up of a group of parishes varying in number depending on the density of the population. These were under the control of a District Commissioner supported by assistants and an organising committee. The District Commissioner was accountable to his County Commissioner for all of the Scout Patrols and Scout Troops in his District and for the welfare of the Movement within the District. This system remains in place to this day, virtually without modification.

CHAPTER THREE

The Early Years Nationally

So why did the sudden explosion of Scouting take place and why did it take B-P, the authorities and even dear old ladies by surprise. The answer in my view is two fold. Firstly the adult view was that there were already sufficient organizations in existence to meet the needs of young boys and that the programme of Scouting offered by "Scouting for Boys" would be taken up and absorbed into their existing training programmes. In North Oxfordshire there were, for example, Boys Brigades, Church Lads Brigades, Church Choirs, Bands of Hope (the temperance movement's youth arm) and of course Public Schools. There was therefore no perceived need or call for a new and separate organisation.

Secondly, the adult's view did not take into account the response to "Scouting for Boys" by the boys themselves. "Scouting for Boys" was after all the work of their hero, and what he was offering was excitement and adventure typified by the illustration on the front cover of the first issue of "Scouting for Boys", which showed a Scout laying flat on the ground, looking out over a cliff at a deserted beach where there was a boat drawn up on the shore and from which men appeared to be carrying contraband from a ship on the horizon. Smugglers! Great excitement indeed.

To become a Scout you didn't have to join an existing organisation; all you needed was to find no more than five friends — sufficient to form a Boy Scout Patrol — and you were in business. You didn't have to meet indoors; you met out of doors which was much more fun. You didn't have to suffer Bible study and you didn't have to involve adults. In addition you were given a set of values in the form of the Scout Law and Promise to which you could relate, and which were all positive, "A Scout is …." rather than the "Thou shalt not…" of the Bible. And above all you did exciting things which no other organisation offered like field craft, tracking and lighting fires.

The Scout Promise

On my honour I promise that I will do my best —
To do my duty to God, and the King,
To help other people at all times,
To obey the Scout Law.

The Scout Law

1. A Scout's honour is to be trusted.
2. A Scout is loyal to the King, his Country, his Scouters,
      his Parents, his Employers, and to those under him.
3. A Scout's duty is to be useful, and to help others.
4. A Scout is a friend to all, and a brother to every other Scout,
      no matter what country, class or creed the other belongs.
5. A Scout is courteous.
6. A Scout is a friend to animals.
7. A Scout obeys orders of his Parents, Patrol Leader,
      or Scoutmaster, without question.
8. A Scout smiles and whistles under all difficulties.
9. A Scout is thrifty.

A tenth Scout Law was added in 1911;
    "A Scout is clean in thought, word and deed."

Scouts took both the promise and law seriously, although this did exclude times when they took a more light-hearted view. For instance the 8th Scout Law; "A Scout smiles and whistles under all difficulties". It could be argued that smiling and whistling at the same time was a difficulty in itself. Try it. Or the 9th Scout Law; "A Scout is thrifty". This was not the age of a Scout nor did "thrifty" lie midway between forty and sixty.

CHAPTER FOUR

The Early Years Locally

So what happened in North Oxfordshire? The answer is that at this point in time we don't know. The problem with researching the history of any voluntary organisation is that its membership is constantly changing and there is also a tendency to retain only those things that are of current interest. This is particularly true of the Scout Movement, added to which it is not the habit of most young boys on returning home after a Scout night to consign the happenings of the night to paper for the sake of posterity.

To discover what happened in the early years of the Movement in North Oxfordshire we have, in the main, to rely on newspaper reports and Scout Headquarters' archives which in both cases are extremely sketchy and intermittent.

The first official reference we have to Scouting in North Oxfordshire is of the issue of a Scoutmaster's warrant to T Hugh Davies of 12 Albert Street, Banbury in November 1909. He was Scoutmaster of the 1st Banbury Boy Scout Troop. Nothing else is known about him. However there is a newspaper report that indicates that the Troop (A Troop is a number of Scout patrols working as a unit) had been in existence for some time before that. In October 1909 the Banbury Advertiser reported that the Troop had been on a visit to Chipping Norton for a Church Parade. Afterwards, together with other Troops including the Chipping Norton Troop they had retired to a nearby field to light fires and cook dinner. After tea they returned to Banbury after an enjoyable day. The article closes by stating that the Troop requires new recruits over the age of 14 to complete a Patrol and that they should apply on Friday 29th October 1909 at 5 South Bar, Banbury. 5 South Bar was (and still is) the photographic studios and shop of Mr Blinkhorn.

The spring and summer of 1910 began to see increased activity within the area.

In the 14th April 1910 issue of the Banbury Guardian there is a report of a combined exercise between the newly formed 1st Bloxham Troop and 1st Banbury Troop in the area around Wykham Lane and Ells Farm Lane, roughly midway between Banbury and Bloxham. This kind of exercise was the forerunner of what became known as a wide game — a game played over a large area of land or within a town or village. This type of game has been greatly enjoyed by Scouts for many years — and still is.

The following week's edition reported that "A cyclist patrol from 1st Banbury with a Scoutmaster attended church parade at Shipton under Wychwood. Starting from Banbury Cross at 7.45 am they had a very rough journey arriving at 10 am. 78 Scouts were on parade from Oxford, Burford, Charlbury, Chipping Norton, Churchill and Banbury. After the service they made their way to a field close by where they cooked their food. Having spent a most enjoyable day the Banbury Scouts arrived back at 8.45pm".

In early June 1910 the Banbury Advertiser carried a report about 1st Banbury's first camp of the year. This camp was also reported in the July edition of "Headquarters Gazette" published by Scout Headquarters (an early publication designed to inform adults within the Movement of its development and to convey instructions on the organisation of Scout Troops etc.). The two reports are slightly different but what is clear is that ten Scouts under the leadership of Scoutmasters T Hugh Davies and F B Hargreaves together with Mr B Taylor left Banbury at 3.00pm on the Saturday and hiked to Pillerton Hersey (A small village midway between Banbury and Stratford upon Avon). Each boy carried provisions for two days together with a blanket and coat. They took tea at Upton House near Edgehill before arriving at Pillerton Hersey where they bivouacked in farm buildings and slept overnight. They woke up at 3.00am and had breakfast (Things have not changed over the years; it is quite common even today for Scouts to wake up early — very early — after their first night's sleep under canvas. However by the end of a week's camp it is extremely difficult to get them up at all. I am sure that the ten Scouts of 1910 would have been no different). After breakfast they were shown around the church and tower by the vicar and then attended church service. At some time over the weekend they met with a Mr W Fletcher who was thinking of starting a Scout Troop in Warmington, a small Warwickshire village on the borders of Oxfordshire about six miles from

Banbury and about three miles from Pillerton Hersey. As a result of that meeting another camp was arranged for three weeks time in Warmington. After church they returned to Banbury stopping for tea at Radway and continuing to Banbury via Hornton and Horley arriving in Banbury at about 7.30pm. They had covered a total of 36 miles during the weekend. The final comment in the Headquarters Gazette was that "The lads stuck to it like bricks".

As arranged, three weeks later the Troop camped at Warmington, whilst there they were inspected at the home of Mr W Fletcher by Lord Willoughby de Broke, owner of Warwick Castle. His lordship was so impressed with the Troop that he invited them camp on his estate at Kineton.

On the Monday after the Troop had returned to Banbury the County Commissioner for Warwickshire, Col Wiggins addressed a crowded meeting in the village at which nearly thirty boys were enrolled as prospective Scouts.

In July 1910 Mr Angus Braggins of Messrs G F Braggins & Co presented 1st Banbury Troop with a kit cart (trek cart). G F Braggins & Co were large timber merchants in Banbury with a large timber yard and manufactory in Gatteridge Street, Banbury who had an extensive gate department producing gates for use by farmers and others. The kit cart was a slightly smaller version of the traditional builders' cart. The kit cart presented to 1st Banbury was, I believe, a prototype cart and its design called on the experience and expertise of the gate department. The Banbury Guardian described it as follows; "The kit cart could be taken to pieces for transport. The sides of the cart when formed together made a fourteen foot ladder. The body could either be used as a camp table or a stretcher and the stretcher could be either carried with or without wheels. The handles fitted into sockets which were screwed up with thumb screws and could be inserted at either or both ends of the cart and in case the handles broke Scout staves could be inserted instead. The ladders were sufficiently strong to bridge a stream 10ft wide." The cart was well received and Braggins & Co went on to sell many such carts to Scout Troops throughout the country. Fortunately, thanks to Dave Sims, formerly of 1st Bodicote, I have a photograph of the kit cart owned by 1st Bodicote Scouts taken in 1957 which is about the same time that I recall seeing one at a scout camp in Wykham Lane. Unfortunately it no longer exists as I am told that it was "burnt" some time later, being somewhat old and decrepit.

During the summer of 1910 two acts of bravery were reported in the local press.

On 20th June a Bloxham lad called Brooks was learning to swim at Wykham Mill when he got into deep water and was drowning. A Scout; Patrol Leader Henry Grinter saw his plight and dived in and rescued him. He then took young Brooks home.

The other incident happened in Brackley which technically is outside of Banbury District as it is in Northamptonshire, but it

The Braggins Kit Cart at a 1st Bodicote Scout Camp in Wykham Lane, Bodicote in the summer of 1957.

was reported in the local press. Apparently at the end of May two suffragettes were being mobbed by an angry crowd in the centre of Brackley when a patrol of Scouts went to their rescue and saved them from the mob. Nothing more would have been heard of the incident but one of the suffragettes wrote to B-P who then wrote a letter to their Scoutmaster in Brackley commending them for their prompt action.

A different kind of incident was reported by the Banbury Guardian on 29th September 1910. It would appear that on the previous Tuesday night, Mr Norman Braggins, a Scoutmaster took to the Town Hall a Boy Scout named Bert Hartwell, aged 15 of Centre Street, Grimsbury, who had received an injury to his back by slipping off the kerb in Castle Street West. He was taken home on the police ambulance having previously been examined by Mr H Beatie. The injuries were such that the boy could not walk at the time.

In September 1910 a Rally and Display was held in the old flower show field which was in the Grounds of Beechfield House in West Bar, Banbury and was well attended by the residents of the town and was commented on favourably by the Banbury Guardian. In addition to the 1st Banbury Troop there were Troops from Brackley, Chipping Norton, Bloxham and Culworth taking part, in total about 80 Scouts. Exhibitions were given of tent pitching, cooking a meal and laying and lighting a bivouac fire. The most effective and interesting

"BE PREPARED"!!
THE SCOUTS' MOTTO.

Under the direction of
CAPTAIN PHILIP HUNLOKE,
Scout Commissioner for Oxfordshire,
Who will be present,

A RALLY OF THE SCOUTS

OF BANBURY AND DISTRICT
Will take place on,

Saturday, September 24th,

At 2.30 p.m., in the
OLD FLOWER SHOW FIELD, BROUGHTON ROAD, BANBURY,
By kind permission of Mr. W. S. Orchard.

DISPLAYS

Will be given of Fire Drill and Rescue from Burning Building, Ambulance Work, Transport and Pioneering, Tent Pitching, and General Camp Life.

ADMISSION—To Grounds, 6d. To Enclosure, with Seat, 1s.
NORMAN BRAGGINS,
T. H. DAVIES,
F. B. HARGREAVES,
Scoutmasters.

Advertisement for a "Rally of Scouts" placed in the Banbury Guardian on 15th September 1910.

event, especially to the young people present, was an exhibition of a burning building with Scouts to the rescue, featuring rescue and fire engine work. There were also displays of kit cart racing over obstacles. However, the most detailed report was to be found in the Banbury Advertiser which is reprinted in full overleaf.

The Banbury Advertiser, 29 September 1910

Boy Scouts Movement
Rally and Display at Banbury

The Boy Scouts' movement has taken root in Banbury and the district as in other parts of the country, and on Saturday, by permission of Mr W H Orchard, there was a rally of Scouts of the town and district in the Old Flower Show Field, Broughton Road. The troops represented were the Banbury, Bloxham, Chipping Norton, Culworth, Brackley and Greatworth, the total strength being between sixty and seventy. The place of assembly was near Bridge Bank, and the lads attracted considerable attention as, in their picturesque uniforms and having with them their kit carts, they marched through the town to the Bath Road entrance to the field. The scoutmasters present were Mr Norman Braggins, Mr T H Davies and Mr F B Hargreaves (Banbury), Mr W Bradford (Bloxham), Mr Lewis (Chipping Norton), Mr J Griffiths (Brackley), and Mr J R Stanley (Culworth); Mr H J Swann and Mr C Woodford (assistant scoutmasters for Culworth and Bloxham respectively) were also in attendance. Captain Phillip Hunloke, Scout Commissioner for Oxfordshire, was prevented by a family bereavement from being present, and his place was kindly filled by Captain Paul RN, of The Highlands, Tadmarton, who was accompanied by Mrs Paul, Miss Paul, and Viscount Tarbert the little son of the Countess of Cromertie, in the uniform of a scout. Among interested spectators of the proceedings were also Colonel Frazer, Captain Yates, Mr J H Blacklock, Mr W I Shaw, Dr Pemberton, the Rev A Jackson, the Mayor of Banbury (Alderman J J Chard), Alderman H R Webb, Mr F J Dalby, Mr O S Marshall Etc. The afternoon was beautifully fine, and it is a matter for regret that the affair was not more largely patronised by the general public. The bright sunlight and woodland scenery forming almost a complete background to the area of operations made a very pleasing scene. The Scouts after arrival on the ground disappeared from view under cover of the plantation, and on the sounding of the "fall-in" they reappeared and formed up in patrols in a semi-circle around the flagstaff. As Mrs Paul hoisted the flag the Scouts came to the salute on the order "Present arms," and the troops having formed into line, Captain and Mrs Paul, accompanied by Scoutmasters Braggins and Lewis, made an inspection of the column, passing up and down the open ranks. Subsequently the Scouts formed up by the baggage wagons, and a cyclist and foot scouts were posted to look out for a camping ground and report. In due time the columns marched to the selected spot, taking with them their equipment, and a party were quickly engaged in pitching two bell tents, while some quickly rigged up sheets to form a bivouac. Others following out directions, brought in straw, wood, and other material for fires, rations, water for cooking etc, sentries meanwhile being posted round the camp. Kindling of fires and preparation of food for cooking went on simultaneously with the performance of ablutions by Scouts who had completed their task. Other phases of camp life were also represented. Some of the Scouts were practising the throwing of life-lines, in which no little skill was displayed, and signalling. Suddenly came an alarm of "Fire!" and instantly the Scouts rushed from their occupations to the scene of the conflagration and after rescues had been affected from the burning building, buckets of water were passed along the line and dashed upon the flames which were fast enveloping the erection specially constructed for the purpose. The ambulance corps were also busily engaged in rendering first aid to the supposed sufferers from the fire and bearing them into camp on stretchers. Meanwhile the Bloxham Scouts' fire engine (a small manual formerly privately owned by the late Mr Denchfield, and subsequently given by Miss Denchfield to the Bloxham Fire Brigade, and by that body transferred to the Scouts) was got into play, and the fire was soon got under, the lads finishing their task by razing the structure to the ground. After this work the Scouts returned to camp, and two selected teams gave a smart kit-cart display. The two carts of the Banbury Troop are the invention and were constructed under the direction of Messrs A and N Braggins, and the different parts, which are easily detachable, are applicable to various purposes, including the bed of the cart as a table and the sides fitting together and forming ladders. The Scouts demonstrated their skill in detaching their carts and taking them over five-barred gates, surmounting

an obstacle from ten to twelve feet in height, and crossing a supposed stream about four yards in width. This display was one of the
most interesting exhibitions of the afternoon, and the spectators
manifested their appreciation by repeated applause. This completed the programme with the exception of the final rally. The Scouts
having been formed up in column, Captain Paul briefly addressed
them. He said that until that afternoon he knew practically nothing
about Boy Scouts, and he was very glad to have been asked to attend
that day's display, because it had shown him what a fine thing the
Boy Scouts was, and he should in future take great interest in them.
He thought that the movements that they had gone through had been
very good indeed. He was very much struck with the way in
which their camp was pitched, and also the display with the kit-
cart - which he thought was a wonderful invention — and the way in
which they had got it across the water. He believed that every British
boy had the desire to do something or other to help his country,
and one of the ways in which he could do it was by learning scouting. As they knew, soldiers were chosen by reason of their pluck and
cleverness to go out as scouts in time of war to ascertain for their
party what the enemy was doing. Besides war scouts there were also
peace scouts, by reason of their mobility, power to understand life
in the jungle, and to learn something from the smallest signs around
them. There had been men who had given up everything to do work
of that kind and they had done very excellent service, because it had
been their duty to their king and country. The empire had been
built up by scouts of that kind. For hundreds of years, from
Queen Elizabeth's time, there had been men, whose names were
familiar to them, who had gone out into different parts of the world
and made discoveries which had been of immense advantage to this
country; and there had been brave women scouts as well, among
them Grace Darling and Florence Nightingale, the last-named of
whom went out to nurse the sick and wounded in the Crimea. From
what they had seen that day he thought that everyone in Banbury
and district should do anything they could for the support of Boy
Scouts. — Mr Lewis, of the Chipping Norton "Pioneers" said they
could not do less than give three hearty cheers for Captain and Mrs
Paul for their presence there that day — There was a hearty response,

followed by the singing of "God save the King" — The general public
then dispersed, and subsequently the Scouts partook of tea in the field.

The Scoutmasters desire to thank all those who in a variety of
ways rendered assistance in connection with the rally and display.

Following the establishment of a national framework for the movement North Oxfordshire was not initially a district within its own right but formed part of a larger Scout District based on Burford. However, following the successful rally in September 1910 steps were taken to establish a Scout District based around Banbury. In January 1911 the Banbury District was established which included all Oxfordshire parishes north of and including Deddington, Swerford and Hook Norton, plus, by arrangement with Warwickshire, Shotteswell. However, for some unknown reason Hook Norton did not become actively involved within

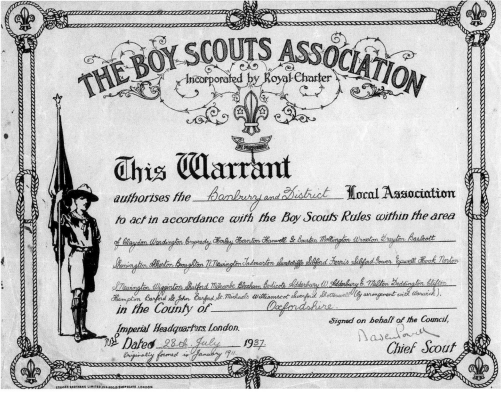

The Warrant recording the registration of the Local Association (The body responsible for managing the affairs of the District) setting out its area of responsibility parish by parish. This certificate was issued on 28th July 1937 but states that the District was originally formed in 1911. Note that there are no specific references to any of the Banbury parishes.

the District. There is no record of a troop having been formed in Hook Norton nor does there appear to be any official records of such a troop which is rather unusual for such a large village. I know that there was a troop in the village in 1949 as a fellow pupil at Banbury Grammar School, Edward Albert George Mobley (Could he have been born at around the time of George VI coronation?) was a member, but at that time they preferred to consider themselves part of Chipping Norton District. It was not until the early 1960s that it took its rightful place within Banbury District.

In the summer of 1910 a Scout Troop was formed in Deddington under the leadership of Rev H Tyrell Green and the members of the two patrols (the Otters and the Peacocks) were invested by Col Murray who said that the Troop could use his land for scout activities. A great deal of fund raising activities took place in the village to raise funds for tentage and other equipment.

In February 1911 according to a return made to Scout Headquarters, the Banbury District consisted of two troops; 1st Banbury and 1st Bloxham with a total strength, including leaders of 67. However 1st Deddington was not included although by that time it was well established. The reason for this omission is, I believe, because in the early days of the Movement boundaries were extremely flexible and also not properly understood. It could be that like Hook Norton it preferred to work with another Scout District, in this case probably Woodstock. There were additionally a number of Scout patrols located in some of the villages around Banbury but these were not brought within the District organisation until a few years later — if they were still in existence.

According to the return to Headquarters the District president was Captain Paul RN of the Highlands, Tadmarton, its Chairman was S Mawle of Broughton Road, Banbury and its Secretary was Thos Blinkhorn of 5 South Bar, Banbury. There was no District Commissioner.

The Blinkhorn family have had a long association with Scouting locally, Thos Blinkhorn was the father of Norman Blinkhorn who was a founder member of 1st Banbury and may well have been one of the ten scouts who took part in their hike to Pillerton Hersey and back and also their trip to Warmington. Norman was an active member and supporter of Scouting until his death and his son Martin was a Scout in 3rd Banbury (County School) Troop in his youth.

By 1911 1st Bloxham was being led by Scoutmaster W Bradford of Banbury Road, Bloxham whose warrant is dated 31st January 1911, assisted by R W Booth of Bloxham whose warrant is dated 16th June 1911. I understand that Mr Bradford was the village schoolmaster and choirmaster.

Today 1st Bloxham may claim with some justification to be the oldest Scout Group in North Oxfordshire although this may be disputed by 6th Banbury who were formed when 1st Banbury was split into two Groups (4th Banbury and 6th Banbury) in October 1970.

The summer of 1911 saw a large pageant to celebrate the coronation of George V, involving most local organisations, which was held on the old showground in Oxford Road (probably where Sainsbury's is today) and Scouts played their part. The Banbury Advertiser lists the Scouts involved as; Mawle, D Braggins, Bliss, Matthews, Jelfs, Salter, A Braggins, Hitchcox, Hatcher, Matthews, Ayres, Aldridge, Hislop, Broodbank, Viggers, Woods, Lewis, Preedy, Lake, Sewell, Castle, Meadows, Gibbard, Harris, Cooling, Wells, Walker, Wilkins, Powell, Turbitt, Blinkhorn, and Bannard. The article concludes with the comment that "The Boy Scouts improve with acquaintance."

In April 1912 the first AGM of the newly formed District was held in the Scout room in Calthorpe Street, Banbury and it was extensively reported in the Banbury Guardian. There were 77 Scouts in the District. New troops were being formed in Adderbury, Tadmarton and Wroxton and Scout patrols in Grimsbury and Bourton. Attempts were being made to start troops in Cropredy and Swalcliffe. The District had £6. 19. 5½d (£6.97) in hand.

On 15th April 1912 the whole nation was rocked by the tragedy of the sinking of the Titanic and Scouts locally helped organise a collection for the disaster fund collecting £12; half of it from Banbury races on the racecourse around Crouch Hill.

In July 1912 the District's first District Commissioner was appointed. He was Mr Francis Fitzgerald of Wroxton who was, I believe, the son-in-law of Lord North of Wroxton Abbey. To a degree this was somewhat of an honorary appointment as he does not appear to have played an active role in the District. More important was the appointment of Norman Braggins as District Scoutmaster. He was responsible for not only the Scout troops but also for the Scout patrols that existed in the District.

1st Banbury Boy Scout Troop posing for a photograph taken by Thomas Blinkhorn outside his shop in South Bar, Banbury in April 1912 following the Titanic disaster. The scouts were collecting money for the Mansion House appeal set up immediately following the disaster. This is the earliest known photograph of Banbury Scouts. Norman Blinkhorn is far left and his brother Bernard is far right. Note that none of the scouts are wearing woggles.

Norman was the uncle of Don Braggins who was a founder member of 1st Banbury and the brother of Angus Braggins. Both brothers worked for the family firm of G F Braggins & Co. Norman was, I believe, largely responsible for the organisation of the Scout rally in 1910.

When Don Braggins was Mayor of Banbury in 1947 he presided over a Girl Guide rally in the Town Hall which was addressed by Lady Baden Powell, B-P's widow. During the course of the rally he mentioned that he had attended a large Boy Scout rally in Windsor Great Park in July 1911 as a member of 1st Banbury Troop.

July 1912 saw 1st Banbury attending a Scout rally in Northampton attended by HRH Prince Alexander of Teck were they built a suspension bridge which the Prince walked over commenting that it was "very well done indeed".

In November 1912 a Scout Troop was formed in Bodicote with Miss Olave Starkey as Scoutmaster. The Starkeys were wealthy residents of the village.

CHAPTER FIVE

The District Flourishes

Throughout 1912 and 1913 the expansion of the District was the result of a great deal of work by Norman Braggins and the District Chairman Syd J Mawle. This work was not limited to Banbury District and often overflowed into Northamptonshire, with them on one occasion, speaking to interested villagers of Kings Sutton at Astrop House.

In 1913 there was great excitement in the District as it was reported that B-P was to visit the town in July following his attendance at a large Scout Rally and exhibition in Birmingham. Unfortunately his visit had to be cancelled due to his ill health.

B-P therefore never visited the District, however we do have substantial connections to him and his family as his eldest daughter Heather and her husband Wing Commander John King lived for many years at South Newington and then for a period of time at Swerbrook Farm, Wigginton. In the 1980s John was president of the District for a number of years. B-P's grandson the present Lord Baden-Powell also visited the District early in the 1980s to attend the Tour de Trigs Walking Competition in the early years of this well established hike. And of course Lady B-P visited the town on two occasions, once in November 1943 and again in April 1947, to attend Girl Guide rallies in the Town Hall, although it does not appear that the Scouts were invited to attend. Perhaps it was because on both occasions there was insufficient room for other than Guides.

Following the success of the rally held in September 1910 another rally was held in June 1913 this time not only to promote Scouting but also to raise funds to send scouts to a large rally in Birmingham in July.

The newspaper report is set out overleaf.

The Banbury Advertiser, 19th June 1913

BOY SCOUT'S RALLY AT BANBURY
Inspection by Lord North
Exhibitions and Competitions

With the objects of demonstrating that the training received by Boy Scouts is practical and useful, to endeavour to waken in this district an active interest in the movement, and to raise funds to defray the expenses connected with the attendance of representative local teams at the great national rally and exhibition to be held at Birmingham during the first week in July, a rally under the auspices of the Banbury and District Boy Scouts' Association took place at Banbury on Saturday afternoon, Lord North (president of the Banbury and District Boy Scouts' Association) attending and inspecting the Troops. The proceedings commenced with a parade of Troops in the Horse Fair, under District Scoutmasters Norman Braggins and J W Griffiths. Headed by the Banbury Borough Band (conducted by Mr G Barnett) the Troops marched to the Britannia Works Recreation Ground, where there were interesting exhibitions and competitions in scout work, illustrations of life in camp, etc, a special feature being the fire drill of the 10th Oxford Troop, which is one of the smartest exponents of this section of boy scout work in the country. For this display the squad brought with them one of the Oxford City horsed manual engines. The attendance of the general public was not so large as might have been expected, and, indeed, hoped for, but this may have been partly due to other attractions in the neighbourhood. The weather, fortunately, was most favourable for such a gathering, and a very interesting afternoon resulted. The Banbury Troop was at nearly full strength, the officers in charge being District Scoutmaster N Braggins and assistant Scoutmaster G Hearn, and the other Troops, with numbers in attendance, comprised the following:- Oxford (10), Scoutmaster K V Carter and Assistant Scoutmaster Alden; Bodicote (21), Assistant Scoutmasters Taylor and Curtis: Chipping Norton "Pioneer" Troop (7), Assistant Scoutmasters A Spencer and Wilson; Charlton (16), Scoutmaster W

Chetwynd; Wroxton (16), Patrol Leader A Wise; Chacombe, Scoutmaster Evins; Edge Hill, Assistant Scoutmaster Hayden; Middleton Cheney (11), Scoutmaster S J Rogers and Assistant E Waters; Tadmarton, Patrol Leader Gibbs; Culworth (10), District Scoutmaster Stanley; Sulgrave (6), Scoutmaster H J Swann; Farnborough (12), Assistant Scoutmistress Miss Holbech; Kings Sutton (20), Assistant Scoutmaster Thorpe. Adderbury Troop was also represented. There were also present Miss Starkey (Scoutmistress of the Bodicote Troop), Miss Carey (Scoutmistress of the Edge Hill Troop), Mr C W Emlyn (Assistant Commissioner for the County of Northampton and District Commissioner for South Northamptonshire), Mr S J Mawle (chairman of the District Committee and hon. Secretary of the Bodicote Troop), Mr T H Blinkhorn (hon. secretary of the Association), Captain Symonds and Fireman Beesley (of the Oxford Fire Brigade) and Dr. Ormrod (representing the Oxford Scouts Friends). The total number of scouts present was close upon two hundred. Lord North was accompanied by Lady North, Mr F and the Hon. Mrs Fitzgerald, Miss Eileen Fitzgerald, and Mr Dudley Fitzgerald. There were also present Lord and Lady Saye and Sele, the Rev. Father Adkins (Newton Abbott), the Rev. Dr.Verrault, the Rev. A E Riddle, the Rev. Tyrell-Green, The Mayor of Banbury (Mr H R Webb) and Miss Webb, Captain and Mrs Yates, Captain and Mrs Paul and Miss Paul, Mr E Samuelson, Dr. F Judge Baldwin, etc.

The programme in the field was commenced with a march past in column of patrols, Lord North being at the saluting point with Mr F Fitzgerald, the Mayor, and Mr C W Emlyn. The Troops marched past twice, to the inspiriting music of the Borough Band, and the movements were very smartly carried out. The boys were afterwards formed up on three sides of a square, and Lord North made a minute inspection of the ranks. The 1st Banbury Troop, under District Scoutmaster N Braggins, next gave an exhibition in bridge—building and pioneering. The river, represented by a canvass sheet, obstructed the advance scouts, who, after ascertaining its width, retired to the main body and reported. Pioneers came forward with derrick poles and ropes, by means of which block and tackle was rigged up and men and baggage conveyed over the imaginary river, a bridge

being afterwards erected sufficiently strong to bear the passage of
the main body. While this work was proceeding, other Scouts were
engaged in pitching tents, attending to the commissariat department, and generally settling down in camp, in which work the lads
displayed great aptitude. The Middleton Cheney Troop, under
Scoutmaster S J Rogers, erected in quick time a portable bridge,
which the boys had designed and constructed in a very ingenious
manner, the framework being also adapted for use in building a
tent. A kit-cart demonstration by teams from the Banbury and
Bodicote troops was another interesting display, the lads racing
their kit-carts over a course with obstacles representing a farm gate,
a 9ft. wall, a stream 12ft. in width. A very realistic demonstration of
fire drill by the 10th Oxford Troop was a feature of the afternoon.
The Troop had been specially trained by Captain Symonds, Chief
Officer of the Oxford City Fire Brigade, who accompanied the Troop
and superintended the display. The horsed manual fire engine lent
by the Corporation of the City of Oxford. The supply of water was
pumped from the river, and while the preliminaries were being carried out previously to the use of the hose, other scouts were using the
contents of patent extinguishers upon an imaginary burning building. The whole demonstration was carried out in an exceedingly
smart manner, and reflected great credit upon all concerned. A fire-
lighting race, for scouts of any age, proved very interesting. Each
scout was provided with six matches, paper, and a billy-can containing one pint of water. Upon a given signal, the scouts rushed to
a heap of faggot-wood, took what sticks they required, and each
proceeded to light a fire and boil the water. These operations proved
very attractive to the visitors, and in the end the winners were: First,
Thomas Low, "pioneer" Troop, Chipping Norton; second, Wilfred
Neville, Wroxton Troop; third, Patrick, "Pioneer" Troop, Chipping
Norton.

There was also a uniform race for scouts under thirteen years
of age. The competitors were formed into a line, and each removed
his clothing with the exception of his shorts, placing the garments in
a heap before him. At a given signal each scout had to dress himself
correctly and run a short distance to the judges. The winners in this
event were Arthur Luckett (Bodicote Troop), Cecil Austin

(Tadmarton), and Charles Ward (Banbury), in the order named. The concluding item on the programme was a "scout rush". Upon a signal from the commanding officer all the scouts rushed towards the flag-pole shouting their various patrol calls, and seated themselves on the ground.

Lord North then briefly addressed the Scoutmasters and Boy Scouts. He said in the first place he wished to congratulate them all upon the muster that day. The muster, taking everything into consideration, and the various things going on at the moment, was a very good one. The Birmingham rally, which was to be very soon, might have interfered with some of them coming. They had made a very creditable muster, and their appearance was extremely good. He was very much pleased with the way they marched past, and he was particularly struck with the way in which they diminished their front when they went round the second march past. He thought everyone must have been struck with the rapidity with which they erected their bridges, pitched their tents, and did other work. It was extremely well done, extremely solidly done, and done with great rapidity. He thought they must congratulate Mr Braggins upon the invention of the kit-cart, for nothing could be more useful (hear, hear). When he (his lordship) was inspecting their ranks he was very pleased to see worn so many badges, which showed the interest the Scouts took in their work, and the way they had done it. He wanted to remind them that they belonged to a very large organisation which had lately sprung up, and which he thought was fraught with good — so much good that it had extended not only all over England, but was beginning to show itself in foreign countries. The promises they had made to keep the Scout law — to be loyal and true to their country, to help all who were in need, and to do it without any expectation or desire of reward — appeared to him to embrace every duty that they owed one to another. Besides all that, their organisation and their drill taught them to rely upon themselves, to know what to do in stress of circumstances, never to lose their heads, and to do everything with quickness and regularity. The Scout Law also taught them to make themselves good citizens — he did not mean inhabitants of a town, but inhabitants of the country. They promised to be loyal to their King, to assist all in need, and to obey and keep the law laid down by their rules. They did not take an oath about that — they did a much finer thing — they did it on their honour — and when man gave his honour it must remain untarnished, and that honour they must keep all their lives. His lordship concluded by remarking that he was very pleased to inspect the Boy Scouts, and he wished them every success. (Applause).

The prizes in the fire-lighting competition and the uniform race, consisting of articles of Scout equipment, were then presented to the winners by Lord North.

The District Scoutmaster N Braggins, addressing the Scouts, said he thought the least they could do was to thank Lord North for his great kindness in coming to inspect them, and he asked them to give his lordship three cheers.

The Scouts rose to their feet, and, with their hats held aloft on their poles, responded with much heartiness, cheers also being given for Lady North.

The royal salute was followed by the singing of "God save the King", led by the band, and the interesting proceedings terminated.

Tea and other refreshments were served during the afternoon by Mr and Mrs H Johnson, of the Catherine Wheel.

The rally was a financial success and as a result Scouts from Banbury, Bodicote, Chacombe, Culworth, Middleton Cheney, Sulgrave, Tysoe, Kineton and Wroxton were able to travel by train to the Birmingham rally.

The Birmingham rally was not a small local affair but one of the largest rallies held to date by the Scout Movement. There were over 18,000 scouts at the rally (The Banbury Advertiser claimed 30,000) from all over the United Kingdom, its Dominions and Colonies and also from Austria, Poland, Germany, Spain, Italy, France, Belgium, Sweden and the United States. The rally was opened by Princess Alexander of Teck and the Scouts were inspected by Prince Arthur of Connaught and, of course, by their chief, B-P.

Visitors to the rally and exhibition were able to see demonstrations of Scoutcraft plus scouts mending chairs and making baskets or soling and heeling shoes. They could see Scout plumbers, electricians, engineers, tailors and carpenters. In the arena they could see displays of cycling and pioneering, Morris dancing, boxing and wrestling and gymnastics

The Banbury Guardian reported extensively on 1st Banbury's involvement as follows;

"At the Scouts' Exhibition held during last week 1st Banbury were bracketed with 4th Derby in the open competition for bridge building and secured 3rd prize for trek cart drill. Scout H Shrimpton won the silver cup for art metal work and also took two diplomas for painting flowers and birds. Patrol Leader G French won the 1st prize in the open class for practical electrical working gaining a £14 scholarship. 1st Banbury won a £10 prize for fire drill. The Banbury team was selected to give a display at the rally at Perry Bar and gave a demonstration of the use of derrick poles.

It is interesting to note that in the trek cart competition teams winning 1st, 2nd, 3rd and 5th prizes were using the cart designed and manufactured by Messrs G F Braggins & Co of Banbury who are supplying their carts to Scouts in all parts of the country."

Clearly 1st Banbury's performance was of the highest standard and they came away from the rally with a considerable amount of pride. After all they could now claim to be one of the best troops in the United Kingdom if not the world.

CHAPTER SIX

The Great War

Scouting continued to expand, however just after the start of the 1st World War Norman Braggins left the area and moved to North Devon where he became District Commissioner, he was replaced as Scoutmaster of 1st Banbury by Norman Blinkhorn and late in 1916 as District Scoutmaster by J H Stembridge, Scoutmaster of 2nd Bloxham (All Saints Public School). By 1916 there were eight troops on the District register; 1st Banbury (Scoutmaster (sm) N Blinkhorn), Wroxton (sm Miss Fitzgerald), Bloxham (sm Miss Hopkinson), Shenington (sm B Stockton), Horley and

2nd Bloxham (Bloxham School) Boy Scout Troop 1916. The Scoutmaster was J H Stembridge (right) and the Assistant Scoutmaster was Mr Alexander (left). Note the immaculate turnout of the Troop and the uniform of the leaders (There was at that time no formal uniform for leaders which resulted in a wide interpretation of what would pass as uniform).

2nd Bloxham at their Summer Camp held in Aynhoe Park, July 1916.

Hornton (sm Rev Buxton), Bodicote (asm B Curtis), and two troops where the Scoutmaster was in the armed forces, Adderbury (sm "on war service") Tadmarton (sm "on war service"). The total membership was 120.

Norman Braggins must be credited with being the driving force behind the expansion of the movement locally in the years 1910-1913. The District grew entirely due to his efforts and his enthusiasm, supported by the District Chairman, Syd Mawle. The District's loss was very much North Devon's gain. However he left behind a legacy which enabled Scouting in the District to continue despite the effects of the war.

It is interesting to note the two female Scoutmasters at Wroxton and Bloxham. It was in 1916 following a long period of agitation that a junior section of the Movement was formed – The Wolf Cubs which tended to be led by women.

In March 1917 the Banbury Guardian announced that from then on it would publish a "Scout News" feature on a regular basis. The announcement was supported by a letter from B-P and other letters from The Scout Commissioner for Ireland, the District Commissioner, Francis Fitzgerald and the District Scoutmaster, J H Stembridge. But like so many similar ventures in future years it did not last for long, however from the few "Scout News" that were published one can get an insight into how a Scout Troop or Wolf Cub Pack operated on a weekly basis. Compared with today when troops and packs meet once a week in those days meetings were held three times a week and sometimes more often; there would be Troop night on one night and training for proficiency badges on another and band practice on yet another, plus, of course, patrol meetings and weekend camps and expeditions.

The 1914 -1918 war had a severe impact on the fledgling movement nationwide and this is particularly true of Banbury District particularly in the later years of the war.

The Government were in many ways unprepared for the 1st World War particularly the nature of modern warfare and the length of the war. They therefore turned to the Boy Scout Movement for help which was readily given. Scouts undertook many roles. Following the declaration of War on Germany by Britain on 4th August 1914, Scouts in Bugbrook, Patishall, Gayton and Blisworth were reported to be guarding railway bridges in their area although there are no reports of Banbury Scouts doing likewise, although they did guard telephone lines. Scouting in Banbury played its part throughout the war and I can do no better than quote from the following newspaper article.

Banbury Guardian, 2nd October 1919.

Banbury Boy Scouts and War Work

Few people, we believe, realise the excellent services rendered by the Banbury Boy Scouts during the war. In the autumn of 1914 when the war began the services of the 1st Banbury Troop were employed in guarding the telegraph lines, helping the Red Cross with the feeding of the troops at the GWR station etc. Many boys, including the Scoutmaster (Mr Robeson) answered the call of duty and joined His Majesty's Forces, so that after a few months the troop had to be disbanded. It was reformed in 1915, and as time went on the Scouts' services were more and more in request and from the spring of 1917 until the cessation of hostilities most of the boys' spare time was spent doing war work. Among other things the 1st Banbury Scouts

have distributed over 25,000 handbills and leaflets for war, municipal and other matters, used their Bugle Band for recruiting marches, supplied buglers for military funerals, collected waste paper and sold the same for charitable purposes, collected over £70 for the Blind Soldiers' Children's Fund, given displays at fetes, helped at garden parties, concerts, lectures, searched for escaped German prisoners, dug gardens for soldiers wives, etc, etc. The Troop has unaided, during the war made about £200 for charity. In the spring of 1918 when the situation was very grave, the authorities asked how many Scouts in 1st Banbury Troop would volunteer for despatch riders and messenger work in case of invasion. The result was that every scout volunteered. Among the honours won by Banbury Scouts are the D.S.C (Distinguished Service Cross), D.C.M (Distinguished Conduct Medal) and the M.M (Military Medal).

The statement "searched for escaped German prisoners" requires some explanation.

In the latter stages of the war German prisoners of war were imprisoned in Banbury at the workhouse in Warwick Road which at that time was on the edge of the town and adjoining the countryside. To make room for them the inhabitants of the workhouse were moved out and housed in other local institutions. The prisoners of war were employed in building the ironstone railway line which ran from the main line just north of Banbury to the iron ore fields around Wroxton. The Banbury Guardian contains a number of reports of escaped prisoners of war, hence the mention in the report of the local Scouts' involvement. This must have been an exciting adventure for the scouts; a form of wide game but this time for real.

Wars create heroes. The Boer War created a hero out of B-P. The 1st World War was no different in that it created a Scout hero in Jack Cornwell, one of Scouting's eleven holders of the Victoria Cross in the 1st World War. Jack Cornwall received his award for his gallantry on board a battleship during the battle of Jutland when despite severe wounds he stayed at his post throughout the battle. He died from his wounds in May 1916. One of Jack Cornwell's close friends and shipmates on board was a local boy, Jack Robeson who was also injured in the same battle and in early 1917 discharged from the Navy. On his return to Banbury he became involved with 1st Banbury as Assistant Scoutmaster and his sister, Phylis became Cub Mistress. They were to become one of the main-stays of the Troop and Pack throughout the remaining years of the war and for a number of years after (At one point they were reported as being "indefatigable" workers for the Scout Movement). Jack was also very active in raising funds locally for the Jack Cornwell Charity which had been formed in his memory.

Despite retaining its numbers in the early part of the war the enlist-ment of so many men and the need for women to bring up families on their own began to take its toll and by October 1918 it was reported that there were only three Troops in the District; 1st Banbury, 1st Bloxham and Bloxham Public School each with a Wolf Cub Pack attached, giving a total membership of about 120 including about 40 Wolf Cubs. The same num-ber as just before the outbreak of war.

Throughout the war Scouting continued; 2nd Bloxham was reformed after a break of several years early in 1916 and in March 1917 1st Bodicote was reformed with C Catch and C Bushrod as Assistant Scoutmasters although it appears to have closed again by October 1918.

In the Banbury Guardian of 10th January 1918 there is a report head-ed "Plucky Scout"; J Hitchcox of 1st Banbury Scouts stopped a runaway horse and trap in South Bar. The reins were loose on its back and the Scout secured them with a hooked stick and brought the horse to a halt. Could this be the same Hitchcox named in the pageant in 1911 or perhaps a younger brother?

CHAPTER SEVEN

Drifting and Competition

Following the war scouting locally was a shadow of its former self and it took a long time for it to recover.

Not so our sister movement the Girl Guides. The Girl Guide movement was started in 1910 by B-P after he had been "cornered" by a group of "Girl Scouts" attending a Boy Scout rally at the Crystal Palace in September 1909 demanding their own movement. Locally, the early years of Guiding are as much wrapped in mystery as the early years of Scouting. However by 1919 reports of their activities began to be reported in the local newspapers and it is quite clear from these reports that Guiding was flourishing. Companies were active throughout the area and many activities (including rallies at Wroxton Abbey home of Lord North and of his daughter, who was the Guide District Commissioner) were reported. Guiding continued to flourish and in 1925 an article and a photograph appeared in the Banbury Guardian of the Guides parading from St Mary's Church, Banbury following their annual Empire Day parade and service. What was unusual about this was the photograph. Photography was a comparatively new development particularly for the Banbury Guardian and had only been used sparingly in previous issues for photographs of local dignitaries or prize animals at local agricultural shows. To show Girl Guides marching was quite a breakthrough!

The report attached to the photograph ended with the words "It would be a happy thing to see the church filled with Scouts and Guides" Unfortunately this wish was not fulfilled for many years until the advent of the joint Scout and Guide St George's Day parades which started just before the second world war. Prior to that there had been the very occasional joint parade.

The success of the Guide movement locally did not go un-noticed by the Scouts. At the District AGM held in January 1920 the District Commissioner, Mr Fitzgerald in effect blamed the Guides for the failure of scouting locally to expand and grow. What he is quoted as saying is "That the new Girl Guide movement has been the means of transferring interest from the Scout movement." But nothing appears to have been done to rectify this situation apart from 1st Banbury Scouts playing some football matches against local opposition (all of which they appear to have lost. It could be argued that at least it taught them to be good losers) and the offer of two cups to be awarded at a Scout boxing tournament which would enable the Scouts to knock the living daylights out of each other.

There was a degree of co-operation between the two movements. In December 1921 a joint Scout and Guide fundraising ball took place at the Banbury Town Hall which was highly successful. But it was not to be repeated. Instead the Guides took over the running of future balls at the Town Hall as their annual fund raising activity. In effect the Scouts were given the "cold shoulder". These balls turned out to be one of the highlights of the local social calendar and were patronised by all of the leading local families; dance bands from London were often engaged and professional dancers were in attendance to demonstrate the latest in dances and dance steps.

In July 1920 Mr Fitzgerald resigned as District Commissioner and Commander C A Cathcart De Trafford of Tadmarton Lodge took over from him. Nothing is known of the new District Commissioner. He does not appear to have been a very active one. He resigned as District Commissioner in 1923. From then until the appointment of Geoffrey Fiennes in 1928 the District was effectively leaderless.

Scouting appears to have bumbled along for the seven or eight years from 1920, each troop or pack running their training programme with virtually no guidance from the District whatsoever. None of the three Scout groups that existed in October 1918 had closed and two groups, 1st Adderbury and 1st Bodicote had been re-opened.

1920 saw the first World Jamboree held in Olympia, London and although there is a reference in a local newspaper report to raising money for this event (I would imagine to fund some local scouts to attend) there is no record of any scout or scouts from the District doing so.

CHAPTER EIGHT

Revival and Expansion

Geoffrey Fiennes, the 19th Baron Lord Saye and Sele. District Commissioner 1928 -1948. From a drawing dated 1935 now on display in Broughton Castle. Reproduced by kind permission of Lord and Lady Saye and Sele.

In March 1928 things took a turn for the better when a new District committee was formed. Captain the Hon. Geoffrey Fiennes, eldest son of Lord and Lady Saye and Sele of Broughton Castle who had been District Secretary since 1925 took on the role of District Commissioner in 1928. This was just the shot in the arm that the District needed and for the next twenty years Geoffrey Fiennes would be the driving force in Scouting locally until his death early in 1949. Due to his enthusiasm, drive and hard work the District prospered under his leadership and it entered the first of its two golden eras.

In November 1928 a Wolf Cub Pack was started at the Primitive Methodist Church in Church Lane, Banbury. Not to be outdone a Scout Troop was started in August 1929 at the Wesleyan Methodist Church in Marlborough Road, Banbury (2nd Banbury (Wesleyan)). Next, in October 1930 a Scout Troop was started at South Newington. This was followed in January 1931 by a Scout Troop at Banbury County School (3rd Banbury). A little later in March 1932 a Wolf Cub Pack was started at the Baptist Chapel in Bridge Street, Banbury (4th Banbury). These were followed by 1st Sibford in September 1932, 5th Banbury (St Johns) in May 1933, 1st Grimsbury (St Leonard's) in June 1933 and 1st Wardington in October 1936. All of these Troops and Packs are recorded in Scout headquarters records. Additionally Groups appear to have been formed during this period at 6th Banbury (St Hugh's), 1st Broughton, 1st Hanwell and Horley, and 1st Shotteswell.

By 13th July 1937 the District registration lodged at Scout Headquarters recorded the following Groups as being in existence; 1st Banbury (St Mary's), 3rd Banbury (County School), 5th Banbury (St John's), 6th Banbury (St Hugh's), 1st Grimsbury, 1st Broughton, 1st Hanwell and Horley, 1st Shotteswell, 1st Sibford, 1st Wardington, 1st Bloxham and 2nd Bloxham (All Saints). Notable by their absence from this list are 1st Bodicote and 1st Adderbury both of which seem to have had much of a stop start existence.

I recall many years ago reading the minute book (now long since vanished) of the District committee which recorded the registration referred to above at its meeting on the 13th July 1937 not so much for recording this registration but for the opening sentence written by the then District Secretary the Rev Fox of Wardington which read "The meeting started promptly 20 minutes late".

Not only did Scout Group numbers grow during this period up to the outbreak of the 2nd World War but so did the activities within the Groups and within the District.

One of the first successes recorded during the time that Geoffrey Fiennes was District Commissioner was by 1st Banbury Wolf Cubs. In June 1928 they came second in a three counties Wolf Cub Competition held at the international scout camp site at Youlbury, Oxford and then in

July 1929 they went one better, winning the County Totem Pole competition, again at Youlbury. The Totem Pole was due to be presented to the Pack in Church House, Banbury by the County Commissioner, unfortunately the Lady Commissioner in Oxford who had care of it went off on holiday abroad and forgot to give it to the County Commissioner for presentation. This was not discovered until all of the arrangements for the presentation had been made and the Cubs advised of the day, time and place for the presentation. So Norman Blinkhorn came swiftly to the rescue and together with Norman Humphris, made a temporary "mock" Totem Pole for presentation and saved the day. Norman Humphris was Scoutmaster with 1st Banbury and worked with his father in a carpentry and joinery business in Beargarden Road, Banbury. Norman was an active member of Scouting locally throughout his long life. He was a very early blood donor and the Banbury Guardian records how, on one occasion, he was called from a Scout parade service in St Mary's church to give blood.

August 1929 saw the Coming of Age World Jamboree at Arrowe Park, Birkenhead. This was visited by 2nd Bloxham Troop and a small detachment from 1st Bloxham together with Geoffrey Fiennes.

In November 1929 Bloxham School Scouts produced a film about Scouting with help from Norman Blinkhorn, who was a professional photographer, and the Scoutmaster L H Sutton, entitled "Wake up and Scream." It was reported that, not to be outdone, the village troop were planning a similar project.

At the beginning of 1930 the District organised a boxing tournament for Scouts in the District. There were two heats planned and then a final. The first heat was held in 1st Banbury's headquarters at Ark House, Banbury in early February. About 100 people attended. The second heat was held at the same venue two weeks later. About 200 people attended. The Finals were held a further two weeks later at the Co-operative garage in Broad Street, Banbury and over 500 people attended. 1st Bloxham Scouts won the majority of the honours. The tournament was repeated in 1931 and a 1st Bodicote Scout, Cyril Watts was a victor in the under 8 stones final held in the Drill Hall, Banbury. His family still have his winner's certificate. In the semi final Cyril lost in the under 7½ stone class, but when the time for the finals arrived a fellow 1st Bodicote scout who was due to fight in the under 8 stones final was unwell and their scoutmaster asked Cyril to take his place which he did — and he won.

1st Banbury Wolf Cub Pack outside Church House, Horse Fair in July 1929 following the presentation of the County Totem Pole which is just visible above the head of the County Commissioner. The adults in the second row are from left to right, Geoffrey Fiennes, District Commissioner, Sir Mortimer Burrows, County Commissioner for Oxfordshire, Mrs Butler, Cub Mistress 1st Banbury, the other lady is unknown but may be Lady Burrows. This photograph was loaned by Cyril Aston who can be seen on the extreme right in the front row. The Scouts and their leaders are from 1st Adderbury Troop.

On the 24th April 1930 a lengthy article appeared in the Banbury Guardian under the heading "This Scouting Rage" by someone claiming to be "White Knot" It is an extremely flowery article containing all manner of literary references. It does however give an insight into Scouting in the District at that time. It speaks about 1st Banbury and its leaders and the achievements of its cub pack. 2nd Banbury gets a mention as newly formed and flourishing. Ron Messer it is claimed "runs" a cub pack at the Primitive Methodist Chapel and 1st Bodicote is said to be smart, recently formed and held together well. 1st Adderbury Cubs are praised but the Troop is criticised quite strongly; it's Scouts being fast asleep and the troop half dead. 2nd Bloxham gets a mention particularly its film making activities. But praise is heaped on 1st Bloxham in bucket loads as the largest group in the County with 77 members. I quote one paragraph

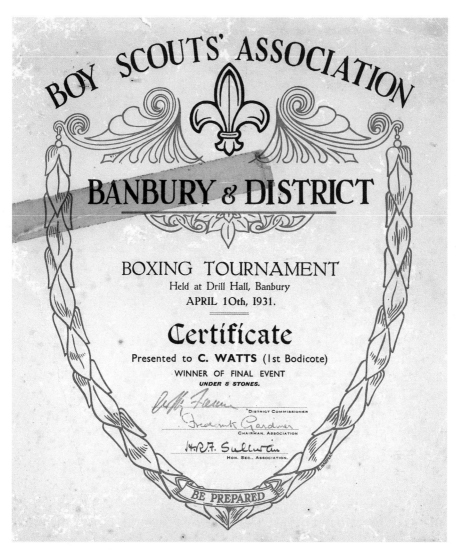

Cyril Watts' boxing certificate for winning the under 8 stone final of the 1931 District Boxing Tournament.

about the Group; "On a Sunday recently the Group paraded, most of them, and those absent were unavoidably so, owing to work etc. The sight of the scarlet and royal blue scarves and the sound of the bugle band coming up the street had its own thrills and its own reasonable glamour."

My feeling is that "White Knot" was a master at Alls Saints School, Bloxham and was involved with the School Troop. The style of language used seems to indicate that he was the same person who wrote an equally flowery article about the World Jamboree at Arrowe Park for the Banbury Guardian a few months earlier.

1st Bloxham Boy Scout Troop outside the village school in 1927/28 complete with their band instruments and drums (the base drum is now in Bloxham village museum). The leaders in the second row are; 5th from left Scoutmaster, Rev J D Ward who was curate to the Rev H T Riddlesdell and also a captain in the Church Army. To his right (fourth from left) is his Assistant Scoutmaster, Fred Mawle who took over from Rev Ward when he left the area and who ran the troop very successfully for many years.

In December 1930 at their annual concert 1st Bloxham showed a film that had been made by their own cinematographic department. The film was shown again in April 1931 and then on the following night shown to the male and female wards at the Horton General Hospital. It would appear that this film was an experiment with a view to doing something more serious as in January 1932 a full length feature film lasting one hour forty five minutes entitled "On the Track" was premiered. It would have been premiered earlier but due to fire in Norman Blinkhorn's studios much of the film was lost and had to be remade. The film was extremely well received by two packed audiences in the Ex-Servicemens' Hall in Bloxham and by the press.

A full report of the film appeared in the 14th January 1932 edition of the Banbury Guardian when the reporter tells his readers that "The theme is that an important document is handed over at Merold Castle (Broughton Castle hall) by the president of a State Conference (Lord Saye and Sele) to Colonel Stercold (Captain the Hon Geoffrey Fiennes) who is called upon to deliver it safely in the land of Acpania. Enemies of that

1st Bodicote Boy Scout Troop in about 1928/29 in the grounds of the Vicarage just off Salt Way, Bodicote. The Scoutmaster is believed to be James Albert Boffin of Farm Place, Bodicote.

land, however, are aware of the diplomatic relations proceeding, endeavour to arrest its progress and, for a time, they do this successfully. As the incidents are unfolded thrilling scenes enhance the filming of the story and as familiar figures were screened the audience applauded. The film justified itself as depicting a story of young life in the Scouting world. An aeroplane is used which is depicted taking part in the endeavour to frustrate the knavish tricks of the enemy against the Wykham Scout Troop, whose star turn is Patrol Leader Jack Fairland (Leslie Clifton). The Great Western Railway and many other agencies have co-operated in the production of this film and altogether it maintained the interest which the promoters anticipated.

It is a story of adventure, fun and scoutcraft and very efficiently staged, as it gives incidents in camp life somewhat detached from ordinary camp scenes."

The report ends with the words "It will be shown at Church House, Banbury, when we hope the local public will take advantage of the opportunity of seeing one of the best amateur films yet produced."

What is not mentioned is that the plot of the film required a "villain" and rather than find one from within 1st Bloxham (Could it be that no one in Bloxham could be that "bad"?) they looked elsewhere and the role was taken by Jim Lewis, an Assistant Scoutmaster with 1st Bodicote whose performance nearly stole the show.

The following report appeared in the local newspaper.

The Banbury Advertiser, 14th January 1932

A LOCAL FILM

Scouts' Screen Success

Well-known residents in a spy drama

Seldom is a real, live peer of the realm seen in the role of a film actor. But this is only one of the many remarkable features of the amateur film "On the Track," which has been produced by local Scouts, and was shown for the first time to a crowded audience at the Bloxham Ex-Servicemen's Hall on Thursday evening. The author and producer is captain J D Ward, of Bloxham.

"On the Track" is not a "talkie," and we can truthfully say that in this case we welcomed the return to the silent film, for one is treated to a full two hours of absorbing thrills and adventures, part of which would undoubtedly have had to be eliminated if the film had not been a silent one. Film fans everywhere have been shouting for action; they have tired of stereotyped screen fare. "On the Track" is crammed with action and thrills, and there is an arresting and enthralling series of sequences. Most people have a liking for the detective type of story, and when one is brought to the screen and served up in so convincing a fashion as "On the Track" it should not be missed, especially when the "detectives" are members of a local troop of Scouts.

It is a splendid story made into a clever picture. Mr N Blinkhorn has acted as technical adviser, which fact in itself would be sufficient guarantee as to the quality of the production.

Some Clever "Shots"

From a technical point of view some of the cleverest "shots" are those showing a GWR express, seen from the window of a signal box, and later as it would appear to anyone lying between the rails. This latter effect was gained by photographing the train from an ashpit between the rails. Some fine up-to-date thrills are provided by an aeroplane chase, in which a Klemm monoplane, which spies are supposed to be using, escapes from three RAF planes.

It is particularly interesting to Banbury audiences to see their own country used as the background for the plot. Glimpses of country near Bloxham, Broughton, and Milton are recognisable, together with Broughton Castle, which has always such an air of romance and drama that it is surprising Elstree producers have not discovered its film possibilities before.

A word must be added in praise of its captions, which are brief and breezy.

If the audience are infected with only half the joys that the boys plainly took in the making of the film, they will have two hours of all stalking, all gripping, all hair-raising entertainment.

The plot is built round the delivery of a diplomatic document by a King's Courier to a foreign land. Enemy spies steal the missive, but are frustrated in their designs by a troop of Boy Scouts.

The Characters

Lord Saye and Sele kindly consented to take part and was eminently fitted to appear as President of the State Conference. As the King's Courier entrusted with the delivery of the package, Capt. the Hon Geoffrey Fiennes is a cool and resourceful diplomatist.

Acting Honours undoubtedly go to Leslie L Clifton, who as Patrol Leader of the Peewits, is a true-to type example of the English Scout — clean, clever and courageous. He survives several harrowing situations, at one time being rescued by the hon. Geoffrey Fiennes, from being cut to pieces on the permanent way, and later being threatened with a revolver while trussed up a tree.

Jim Lewis, 1st Bodicote Troop, very cleverly undertakes the unpopular role of the chief enemy spy, and makes the inhuman callousness and determination of that desperate character appear almost natural.

Valentine Walton and Gordon Heath also give very good performances, whilst Mr Frederick Mawle is all that can be desired as the Scoutmaster.

Other well-known residents of the district who appear in the film include Mr JW Dunne, Major S P Yates, Captain F Gardiner, and Colonel G H Stewart Browne, CB., JP.

The film does the highest credit to Captain Ward and Mr Blinkhorn, and those taking part in its production. The agencies which assisted were the GWR Co., The Chief Constable of Oxford, Lord Willoughby de Broke, MC., MFH., who lent his aeroplane, the Royal Air Force at Heyford, especially Group Captain C I Carmichael, DSO., AFC., and the Air Ministry, Lord Saye and Sele, and others.

The Cast

The full cast is as follows:-

President of the State Conference, The Lord Saye and Sele, Secretary to the Conference, J W Dunne. Colonel W Stercold, King's Courier, member of HM. Diplomatic Corps, Capt. The Hon. G T Fiennes. JP., DC. Jack Fairland, Patrol Leader of the Peewits, Leslie L Clifton, PL. Members of the Conference, Major S P Yates, MC., Capt. F Gardiner, Col. J Ormond, Col. G H Stewart Browne, CB., JP., the Rev. A Robins, MA. (Oxon). Tom Ready, PL. of the Golden Plover Patrol, R D Green, PL. Donald Paignton, Gordon Heath, PL. Boy in the Hedge, Valentine Walton, Patrol Second. Spies and Enemies of Acpania, James Lewis, ASM., 1st Bodicote Troop; Charles Henry Pell, ASM., 1st Bloxham Group; Arthur Hosband, Drum-Major, 1st Bloxham Group; Ernest Callow, Wykham Patrol, 1st Bloxham Group. Brother Bill, William Southam, RSL. The Scoutmaster, Frederick Mawle, SM. The Superintendent of Police, Mr Leonard Bridges. Sergeant, Audley Fisher, Haig Patrol, 1st Bloxham Group. Tim Toyning, Harold Hall, 1st Bloxham Group. Brother Harry, H Neal, ASM. The Troop Leader, Thomas Heath, Group Treasurer and Troop Leader, Bloxhams. "Nucy," Albert Mawle, Patrol Second. Others: M J Hirons, J Phillips, R Harbour, R Hayward, etc. And the 1st Bloxham Group in general.

The Presentation of Certificates.

At Thursday's exhibition of the film Lord Saye and Sele presided, and amongst those present were Lady Hammond Graeme, Miss

Ramsden, the Hon. Geoffrey Fiennes, JP., DC. The Hon. Mrs McLean and Miss Hopkinson, Major Eric Crossley, OBE., Mrs Crossley and Miss Crossley, Major S P Yates MC., and Mrs Yates, Major A G Haigh, Mr and Mrs A R Philippi, Mr and Mrs Ashley and party. Mr and Mrs C L Fortescue, Captain and Mrs F Gardiner, Captain and Mrs H R F Sullivan and party, and Captain E B Johnson.

Apologies for inability to attend were received from Sir Montagu Burrows, Oxford, Lord Willoughby de Broke, and Major A J Edmondson, MP.

During the interval Lord Saye and Sele briefly addressed the audience and afterwards presented Certificates to the following for outstanding work in connection with the film: Leslie Clifton, Patrol Leader, Montagu John Hirons, Thomas Heath, Robert Dennis Green, Gordon Heath, and James Lewis.

Captain Gardiner proposed a vote of thanks to his Lordship for taking the chair and for presenting the certificates. They were all very grateful to him, he said, for lending his support, and also for allowing Captain Ward and the Scouts the use of Broughton Castle.

In seconding, Major Yates said the film had shown them a little of the interest which Lord Saye and Sele took in its production. They all owed him a deep debt of gratitude.

The motion was carried with great acclimation.

Mr Philippi complimented Captain Ward and the Scouts on the magnificent display which had been shown that night.

In reply, Captain Ward paid a high tribute to Mr Blinkhorn's very able assistance in the production of the film and still more in the presentation of it. He appreciated very much the way in which the Scouts had rallied round him after the destruction of the film by fire in September and inspired him to start on a new venture, which was certainly a risk from many points of view. It was due to the loyalty, steadfastness and sacrifice of the Scouts that they had seen what they had that night.

What happened to this film? The answer is we don't know. Geoffrey Fiennes is reported to have said when speaking at later showings of the film that a copy had been sent/sold to Scout Headquarters as part of their film library. However on enquiry at Headquarters they say they can find no record of the film in their archives. It would therefore appear that the film has gone missing and is lost forever. Unless of course you know differently in which case please let me know.

Scouting continued to flourish during the 1930s and by 1933 the District membership had reached 338.

The District Sports was becoming a regular annual feature which was held at various locations throughout the District. Separate sports days were held for the various sections often on a farmer's field but in 1934 they were combined into one event on the Harriers Sports Ground in Banbury,

The District Flag camping competition (which may have started as early as 1920) for scout patrols continued to be held, although towards the end of the 1930s it began to be dominated by the 3rd Banbury (County School) Troop who kept on walking away with the honours.

In 1934 the District acquired its own training ground at Broughton Grounds Farm and over the next year or so proceeded to develop it. In May 1935 a camp chapel, built by scouts of 3rd Banbury under the direction of their Scoutmaster J R "Tec" Railton, was dedicated. The site was primarily used for Scouter training rather than as a scout camp site. What happened to this site and when it fell into disuse is unclear although in all probability it stopped being used during the 2nd World War and the site then returned to agriculture.

By 1936 it is reported that there were fourteen active Scout Groups in the District although it is not clear whether this is the number of troops and packs or the number of groups. My feeling is that it is the former rather than the latter.

Whilst most Troops continued to hold summer camps in England, 3rd Banbury (County School) Troop were much more ambitious, their camps being held hiking in Europe. For example in 1934 they were in the Vosges Mountains in France and in 1935 in Belgium and Luxembourg where they did a complete circuit of Luxembourg. These hike camps, starting in 1931, continued until the outbreak of the 2nd World War in 1939. Following each hike a report was written which was printed in the Group's newsletter "Campfire" and sometimes published in the Banbury Guardian.

Set out overleaf is the report written following the Troop's summer expedition to the Alps in July/August 1937 and which was published in the local newspaper.

Banbury Guardian, 12th August 1937

BANBURY SCOUTS IN THE ALPS

County School Boys' Adventures at High Altitude

A record created in Alpine passing

The annual hike of the Banbury County School Scouts was brought to a successful conclusion on Monday morning when the party arrived safely at Banbury station after a journey in the Swiss Alps, much more exciting and adventurous than any preceding series, and Banbury Scouts have set up an Alpine record by crossing the Blumlisalp and the Hohturli Pass with trek carts and full kits, which has never been done before, and which they were told by the professional guides was impossible.

The party consisted of sixteen, of whom seven were present members of the School. We have received the following report from the hikers.

Leaving Banbury at 6am on July 26th, we arrived at Thun in Switzerland at about 9.30 next day. Here we donned our heavy mountain boots, assembled the trek carts, and set off in search of adventure. As we were tired after the long journey, we only did about six miles that day and camped at Reutigen, under the side of Niesen.

Next day we tackled our first climb — over the Langenberg — a mere 4,600 feet, and down into the Simmerthal. This was not a difficult climb, there was a fair track all the way, though, to be sure, it was mainly loose stones, which gave a poor foothold, and our lungs and hearts, as yet unaccustomed to mountain air, made the task of hauling trek carts rather a strenuous one. We camped at Oey, and, to assist the breaking-in process, kept to the valley next day, moving up the Diamtigthal to Grimmialp. Here we swung east into the foothills of a lofty range which cut us off from Adelboden, our next objective. The pass here is some 7,000 feet up. By midday we had risen above the tree line and were soon in the region of loose scree — shattered stone — bare of vegetation. By this time we had met our first snow, patches in sheltered places, and had a snow fight. After lunch, we tackled the final climb to the summit.

As we reached the top — a real knife-edge — the sight that met our eyes made us all gasp. Below, some 5,000 feet down was the valley, dotted with chalets and seamed with gleaming water-courses. When we looked further, and in front, rank upon rank, rose shining white peaks of the majestic Jungfrau and Blumlisalp range.

Before we could grasp it all, a sudden cloud swept up from the valley, and within thirty seconds all was blotted out; we could see no more than fifteen yards ahead. The sudden disappearance of the sun, burning hot a few minutes before left us all chilled. We sat down on the bare rock, hoping the clouds would clear, and feeling very isolated. In ten minutes' time the range of vision improved, so, roped up in two parties — as it was our first big descent, and cloud was about, we decided to take this precaution — we started the climb down. The valley seemed very near, surely we could reach it in half an hour, or an hour at the most! But the hours passed by, to the accompaniment of the rattle of falling stones, the screech of nails biting bare rock, and it was 8.30 before we reached the road below, just as darkness fell - the mountain walls cutting off the light make the valley lands dark very early. Fortunately we found a shop and an obliging shopkeeper, who not only allowed us to on her land but also invited us to cook in her kitchen.

Next morning early we set off for another climb — over the Bonderkrinden Pass (7,800 feet) to Kanderseeg. The climb at first was gentle. We passed the great Bonder Falls, crossed the forest belt, and were just emerging from it when a thunderstorm broke, round, above and below us. As the storm increased, and clouds thickened, we thought it wise not to attempt the Pass, and camped for the night, just above the tree line. All night the rain continued — rather a restless night for most of us. First we heard the Alpenhorns sounding from the distant chalets below us; then a herd of some fifty cows, each with its bell (some of the bells are ten inches high), insisted on examining the camp, despite our protests, sampling the contents of the cooking gear, falling over tent guys, and generally making a nuisance of themselves all night.

Next morning brought no improvement in the weather. The downpour continued, and a river bed, dry when we first saw it, was now filled with a roaring torrent of icy water. In case of such a misfortune, we carried with us provisions for one day or more, but as the weather showed no signs of improving the SM left the camp at about 2pm. and dropped down the mountain side in search of further supplies. Happily the rain ceased next morning, though the clouds still lingered, and we decided to move on. We crossed the grass belt, and came on to the scree. Here the surface was so bad that we found it better to unload the trek carts and carry the loads over, pushing and hauling the empty carts. We reached the summit at midday, and began the rather tricky descent — tricky because the storm had left the surface loose and treacherous, and in places torrents had entirely washed away the path, leaving awkward gaps on the mountain side. Grunting, sliding and staggering over the loose scree, we got down without mishap, and at 5pm. turned into the gate of the International Scouts Chalet at Kandersteg, where we camped for the night. Luckily, we happened to strike the night of the national festival, and most of us went with many other Scouts at the Chalet to join in the fun in the village.

The next day was a great one in the annals of the Troop. We achieved the crossing of the Blumlisalp and the Hohturli Pass, with trek carts and full kit, which, we were told, had never been done before, and which the professional guides told us was quite impossible. Leaving Kandersteg at 10am, we worked up a stiff gradient to the Oeschinen See, a glacial cirque lake about a mile across, some 5,000 feet above sea level. Rounding this, we climbed on until we came to what appeared to be an endless rock wall, some 150 feet high. On investigation we found a narrow zigzag stairway up the rock face, and after much toil and some delay found ourselves on gassy slopes above the tree line. We met various parties of climbers, all of whom were sure that we should be unable to get over.

By 2.30 we were on the scree, still climbing. At 4.30 we reached the edge of the Kander glacier. Working along the scree at its edge, with the tumbled chaos of green ice beside us, we sighted the Alpine Club hut on the summit of the Pass, and wormed our way towards it. At this height the rarefied air slows one down considerably, and progress was not rapid. At 6.15 the leading party reached the tiny plateau on which the hut stands. It is perhaps worthy of mention that, exhausted as they were after their climb, three boys of this party immediately threw off their packs and returned down the slope to help those who were below — not an easy thing to do! A quarter-of-an-hour later we commenced the descent, anxious to reach the grass before darkness fell. Scrambling through scree and snow, we reached a more or less level grassy patch by 8.30, and camped by a deserted chalet, where we were lucky enough to find sufficient fuel to cook our meal.

The next day we dropped another 5,000 feet down the slope, and worked down the gorge of the Dienach towards Lake Thun, then east towards Interlaken. Some five miles short of this town, we were able to find a camp site in which we could stay for a couple of days, so we made our base while we did our "present hunting" shopping in Interlaken. On the Saturday Morning (August 7th) we boarded a lake steamer which took us down a zigzag course of some 30 miles to Thun, and we camped near the town. Since we would have to rise at 3 next morning, to catch our train home, we turned in early, but got little sleep. Thun had arranged a festival evening, and at 9.30 we were roused by the thunder of many rockets. The sky was lit up for hours, and the noise, intensified as it rolled back from the mountains, made all sleep impossible.

The usual hike report was given at this camp. It should be remembered that this hike is not "foreign travel" nor a sight-seeing tour. It is definitely a Scout Training Camp, and service, self-responsibility and courage in adversity are its main lessons. Each year, if a sufficiently high standard is reached, a hike trophy is awarded, intrinsically valueless, but a recognition of high endeavour, and encouragement for future achievement, and a standard to be aimed at, admitting the recipient to that very small band of holders of the trophy — now eight in number. This year, the report placed Scout K Field, and Rovers J G Jones and P A Harrison in the post of honour. But these already hold the trophy, and so were not eligible again. The award was therefore made to King's Scout R Stevens. Good luck to him — may it inspire him to live up to the honour thus achieved.

The weather was fine throughout, except for three days and the temperature was usually 86 to 90 in the shade.

Thus ended another hike, with its difficulties and hardships,

its comradeship and inspiration. Yet — lest we feel inclined to think too highly of ourselves — the route followed was one which the Swiss National officials describe as "quite safe and straightforward," and — humiliating thought, after our efforts, - one over parts of which the Swiss father will commonly take his wife and children for a day's climb!

The hike was arranged and conducted by Assistant Commissioner J R Railton, Scoutmaster of the County School Troop.

May 1937 saw the coronation of King George VI and King Scouts from the District under the leadership of Scoutmaster Norman Humphris attended. The contingent was made up of Troop Leader A R Harris, Scout Stevens, Patrol Leader Boone and Patrol Leader Bickley all from 3rd Banbury, together with Patrol Leader Bishop from 1st Hanwell and Horley. Whilst in London they met and had a short talk with B-P.

At the District AGM in December 1937 it was reported that there were twelve Groups in the District a decrease of two on the previous year. It was also reported that the District had been offered its own headquarters in the form of the ground floor of the Old Malt House in Old Parr Road, Banbury. The District was to be offered the property on a ten year lease at 5/- (25p) per year. Work would be required to bring the building up to a useable level and it was estimated that it would cost in the region of £100 to £150. An appeal was made for funds.

In February 1938 Banbury Rotary Club decided "to take up" the Scout Movement locally. What this meant is not clear; however at the same meeting where this decision was taken Howard Chapman the Scout District Secretary and also a Rotarian spoke about the new Scout Headquarters and the need to raise £150. It may well be that "taking up" involved providing some of the money required. Rotary and its junior section Round Table has always been supportive of the Movement locally and for many years they have helped with the raising of funds to send Scouts to World Jamborees and other ventures. Perhaps this is what is meant by "taking up". Whatever it means their support has always been greatly valued.

As a result of having a District headquarters the District was able to start what is known as an "open" Group in town i.e. one that is not supported by a particular church or school. The Group was 7th Banbury (Woodland) which started with a cub pack, scout troop and rover crew. The Group Scoutmaster was G Forsyth Lawson (an architect and member of the local Caledonian Society), he was also Scoutmaster and Rover leader, the Cubmaster was H F Golding (later, after the 2nd World War, to become District Commissioner).

One of the traditions in North Oxfordshire is the joint Scout and Guide St George's Day Parade. These were started By Geoffrey Fiennes, Lord Saye and Sele in about 1938 and have continued every year since then — even through the 2nd World War — with the exception of two years; one in 1980 when an unseasonable snowstorm (blizzard) disrupted the electricity in St Mary's Church and made the parade assembly area in Castle Gardens car park unusable, and more recently in 2005 when the District Commissioner cancelled the parade at short notice, much to the annoyance of Scout Groups and Guide Companies, because of decoration work being carried out in the parish church despite other venues being available.

CHAPTER NINE

The Second World War

The 2nd World war had a disastrous effect on Scouting in the District in much the same way that the 1st World War had had earlier. However Scouting did continue albeit at a very much reduced level. In a report produced shortly after the end of the war it states that "the war disorganised Scouting badly locally and most of the Scouters were not available, whilst those who remained were busy with ARP. (air raid precaution) work, Home Guard etc." The opportunities for war service work by Scouts were far less than during the 1st World War due to the better organisation of the civilian population by the Government. Scouts did however get involved in the collection of newspapers much as they had done in 1914-18. In 1942 1st Adderbury were presented with a first aid box by R C Ashmole of Nell Bridge Farm in appreciation of their assistance during harvest. At the District AGM in April 1945 (the first since 1938) Tec Railton reported that scouts in the District had been deeply involved in war work and had carried out thirty types of different jobs. During the war two new Scout Groups were started; 1st Sibford, and 2nd Wardington (Ealing College) who had been temporarily evacuated to Wardington for the duration of the war. Another Troop was also started in Ruscote; 1st Ruscote. The advert announcing its proposed formation referred to it as an Air Scout Troop which would meet in the Air Training Corps headquarters in Ruscote and was in fact a junior section of this organisation aimed at boys not old enough to join the Air Training Corps. By the end of the war it had ceased to exist.

In January 1941 B-P Died at his home in Kenya, he was 83 years old.

Immediately following his death a memorial service was held in St Mary's Church. Present were the DC., Lord Saye and Sele, the ADC., J R "Tec" Railton, and the following Group Scout Leaders, Rev Fox (Wardington Sea Scouts), N Humphris (1st Banbury), R Tuckey (1st Shotteswell) and F Mawle (1st Bloxham) plus over five hundred present and former Scouts and Guides.

Despite the difficulties that the war created Scouting continued. Camps continued to be held locally, Scouts were invested as Rover Scouts at Broughton Castle and the District Flag continued to be competed for.

By the end of the war the only Scout Groups still operating were 1st Banbury — but only a Wolf Cub Pack, 3rd Banbury Scout Troop, 2nd Bloxham (All Saints), 1st Wardington now renamed Upper Cherwell (North Oxon) Sea Scouts and 1st Sibford.

CHAPTER TEN

Post War Recovery

Unlike after the 1st World War Scouting did not stagnate locally but grew steadily throughout the remainder of the 40s and into the 50s. In many respects the growth was more by dissent than by consent although such a phrase may convey the wrong impression it does indicate the nature of growth.

In November 1946 2nd Banbury (Methodist) Scout Group was reformed by Harold Hobbs who had been a Rover Scout in 1st Banbury

2nd Banbury (Methodist) Scout Troop's first summer camp at Penrhyn Bay, near Llandudno. Back row from left to right. B Darlow, D Partridge, Ben Wilson (Scoutmaster), Colin Wain (Assistant Scoutmaster), F Timms, R Newell, B Stone. Middle row, E Pheasant, Master Wilson, A Lampitt. Front row. J Neal, C Partridge, Brian Wilson, S Richardson.

7th Banbury Birthday/ Christmas party in the Co-op Assembly rooms , Broad Street, Banbury in 1949. The leaders in the third row are; Not known, Cyril Watts, Mrs Wilson, Ben Wilson (Group Scout Master) Norman Humphris, Reg Thomas, Geoff Powell, not known, Mr Wild. In the background to the right, proudly displayed, is the District Flag which was won at the District camping competition earlier in the year.

before the war. Initially this was just a Scout Troop but a Wolf Cub Pack was started shortly afterwards. The Scoutmaster was Ben Wilson who was a dispensing pharmacist but after about a year he left to form his own Scout Group, 7th Banbury which met initially in the front room of a private house in Boxhedge Road, Banbury and then later in the Unitarian Chapel in Horse Fair, Banbury. Ben was joined by two other leaders Reg Thomas and Ted Davidson. A change of jobs meant that Ben had to move from the area in 1952. Reg Thomas took over the running of the Group and after a short while in late 1954 Ted Davidson decided to leave and start 1st Bodicote. In the meantime Colin Wain who had taken over as Scoutmaster at 2nd Banbury following the departure of Ben Wilson also left after a few years to form, with Fred Jamieson and Jack Beesley 1st Grimsbury.

The three most influential Group Scout Masters of the late 1950s taken at the joint summer camp between 2nd Banbury and 7th Banbury at Christchurch in the summer of 1954. The three gentlemen are (from left to right) Ted Davidson (at this point in time he was still a Scouter with 7th Banbury but left shortly afterwards to form 1st Bodicote which he led with great success for many years), Vincent (Vic) Parry, Group Scoutmaster 2nd Banbury and Reg Thomas, Group Scoutmaster 7th Banbury. Between them the three Groups; 1st Bodicote, 2nd Banbury and 7th Banbury represented around 80% of the District's membership.

It is interesting to note that all of the four Groups mentioned above continue to exist and during the last 50 plus years have had a considerable impact on Scouting and on the local community.

Between 1946 and 1954 there were further changes; 1st Banbury closed. Ron Vallender who had been running the pack for many years finally gave up the struggle (He was profoundly deaf and had a speech impediment) and transferred his few remaining cubs to 2nd Banbury and joined them as a Scouter. 1st Sibford closed as did the Wardington Sea Scouts. This left just 3rd Banbury (County School) and 2nd Bloxham (All Saints) of the Groups that had survived the war. This was a low point for Scouting locally with a membership of only 247 at the end of 1954 compared with well over 300 before the war. During that time 1st Adderbury

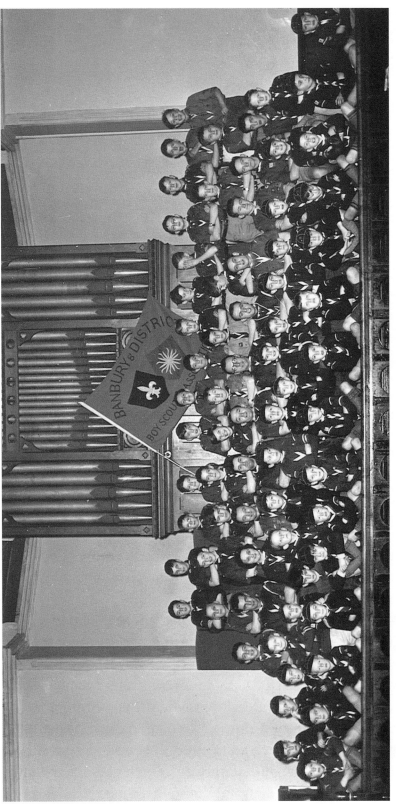

2nd Banbury (Methodist) Birthday Party believed to be in December 1953. The adults in the third row are (left to right) Wilf Pyne, Colin Wain, Mrs Moore, Ron Vallender, Bob Green, Vic Parry (Group Scoutmaster) John Pyne, David Partridge, Tom Pratt, Trevor Parry, Peter Shervington and John Moore. The photograph was taken on stage of the School Room of Marlborough Road Methodist Church. Displayed at the back of the photograph draped across the organ is the District Flag won earlier in the year at the District camping competition by a patrol led by Wilf Pyne and trained by Tom Pratt.

Queen Scouts photographed in 7th Banbury's headquarters at the Jolly Weavers in South Bar, prior to attending the National St Georges' Day Parade and service at St Georges Chapel, Windsor Castle. April 1953. Back Row (left to right); Trevor Parry, David Alder and Peter Shervington (2nd Banbury). Front Row (left to right); Peter Whitehead, Brian Key, and Alan Wild (7th Banbury).

reopened and was highly successful but for some reason closed suddenly just over a year later. I was told that the Scoutmaster had "run off" with the funds, but that may well be no more than misinformed rumour. A troop was also restarted in Shotteswell run by Reg Tuckey but this only survived for a short while.

In 1948 Geoffrey Fiennes who by now had become Lord Saye and Sele following the death of his father resigned as District Commissioner due to ill health and in his place Tec Railton took on the role. Tec had for many years run successfully the 3rd Banbury (County School) Troop and had led them on their numerous excursions into Europe before the war. He had also been Assistant District Commissioner to Geoffrey for several years.

Geoffrey Fiennes died in February 1949. In the 1948-49 District Gazette, (the only year for which such a publication was printed) Tec paid a fitting tribute to him which I quote; "His life and example personified the Scout spirit, he was a source of inspiration to many and will

1st Bodicote's 3rd Birthday Party, 30th November 1957 held in Bodicote Village Hall on the village playing fields adjacent to where the Group built their headquarters. The adults in the second row are (from left to right) Dave Sims, Peter Davidson, Jim Lewis, Bert Golding (District Commissioner) Bill Genese, (Scout Headquarters Staff, Field Commissioner), Ted Davidson (Group Scoutmaster) Kenneth Anderson (County Commissioner), Gilbert Pontin, Cliff Wightman, Janet Edyvean, Jennifer Allen, Mrs Stanley. The District Flag is just visible above Pete Watt's head (back row, 3rd from left) and the County Pennant (presented to the winners of the County Camping competition) is also just visible above "Tub" Yates head (Back row, 4th from right).

always be remembered with affection and gratitude by all members of the Movement. On his retirement, the Chief Scout granted him a warrant as Honorary Commissioner, and awarded him the Meritorious Service Medal and Long Service Decoration."

The Saye and Sele family have had a long association with Scouting. The present Lord Saye and Sele's grandfather the 18th Baron Lord Saye and Sele was president of Oxfordshire Scouting and may well have been its very first president. He was also president of Banbury and District, a matter over which he probably had little choice as his eldest son Geoffrey was its District Commissioner. Following his retirement as District Commissioner due to ill health, Geoffrey then became president of the District and remained so until his death in 1949. His younger brother Ivo followed him as District President.

Broughton Castle and its parkland, particularly during Geoffrey's lifetime, was in many ways a home from home for Banbury Scouts. Not only was the parkland used but so were some of the outbuilding; the first floor rooms over what is now the tea rooms were both a Rover Den and also storage space for camping equipment. The room above the arch in the entrance tower was used by both Scouts and I believe also by Brownies as a meeting room. And of course the castle kitchens were a source of drinking water for those camping in the park.

I remember as a young, new, ten year old Scout in 1948 camping at the back of Broughton Park and collecting our water in canvas buckets from the castle kitchens; great fun going downhill to collect the water but no fun at all on the way back uphill as it was virtually impossible to put a canvas water bucket down without spilling some or most of its contents, which meant another trip to the kitchens.

The author at his first camp, Broughton Park, Easter 1948. This was a cold introduction to camping as in the mornings there was ice on the water buckets.

Geoffrey Fiennes in camp in the late 1920s.

I did, I believe, once met Geoffrey. I recall at one of our camps in the park hearing some of the older Scouts talking quite excitedly about the fact that "Lordy", as Geoffrey was affectionately known, was going to attend our campfire that evening.

Evening came and the camp fire was lit when a group of people appeared through the gloom carrying between them a figure in a wheel chair wrapped up in a huge swath of blankets. It was Lordy, who had been brought to the camp fire by his devoted servants who had carried him in his wheel chair across the park from the castle just to be at the camp fire. Lordy died shortly afterwards but I do not think that my singing played any part in his demise. I like to think that the two people who led the District in each of its two golden eras did in fact, albeit unknowingly, meet.

I recall some time ago talking with the present Lord Saye and Sele about his uncle Geoffrey and he told the tale of how one day whilst escorting a party of visitors around the castle and having arrived at the great hall he noticed that one of the party was not paying any attention whatsoever to what his Lordship had to say (which once upon a time would have been a hanging offence). The elderly gentleman in question was walking around the hall looking up at the ceiling and walking so as to stand immediately underneath a ceiling boss, stopping and looking around before moving on to the next ceiling boss. His Lordship's curiosity got the better of him and so he went up to the old man and asked if he could help. "No" came the reply "You see when I was in the Boy Scouts we camped in the park and the weather was so wet that Lordy invited us all into the great hall to sleep and I am trying to find the ceiling boss that I slept under." Cyril Watts, one of the winners in the 1931 scout boxing tournament, in his memoirs written for his family tells how as a young scout he went to summer camp at Freshwater Bay, Isle of Wight which Geoffrey led. Some time after, his mother told him that Geoffrey had paid for the cost of his camp. Ninety seven year old Arthur Hosband tells how when he was in 1st Bloxham in the 1930s Geoffrey took a small party of scouts from the troop on a cycling holiday to the south coast, unfortunately Arthur and his brother did not have bicycles so Geoffrey went to a cycle shop in Banbury and acquired two (whether they were hired or purchased Arthur does not know) enabling the brothers to join the cycle ride to the south coast. Such acts were typical of Geoffrey and it is no wonder that when he died many a tear was shed. There are numerous tales told by those who knew him of his kindness and of his enthusiasm for the Movement and his untiring work in promoting the ideals of the Scout Laws and Promise.

Throughout the 1950s Scouting continued successfully although with the exception of 1st Bodicote and a small Wolf Cub Pack in Shenington there were no village Groups. The District was quite active and initiated a number of new events.

Tec Railton retired as District Commissioner around 1953 and for a short while the District was without a leader, however Harold Hobbs and Norman Humphris filled the role admirably. Bert Golding became District Commissioner in 1955.

In November 1953 a Group was started in Deddington but by 1956 it

The 2nd Banbury football team, first winners of the Newton Peake Cup (the District football competition) in the 1949-50 competition. From left to right. Back row; D Alder, H Blencowe, P Clack, Not known, J Wyatt, Centre (holding football) C Carter. Front row T Parry, R Darlow, J Barker (captain), R Turner, C Andrews. Notice that there are eleven members of the team but only ten medals.

appears to have closed. It is quite strange that it took so long for Scouting to return to Deddington as it is such a large village. Fortunately the group was not closed for long and it reformed in 1957 and has continued in existence since then; a period of over 50 years.

One of the first District activities organised after the war was a District Scout football competition. A cup was presented to the District by local dentist H Newton Peak who was a supporter of the Movement and also a founder of the local Air Training Corps. The competition was named after him. Every Troop in the District took part in the Competition which ran for many years.

During the 1950s three "Gang Shows" were staged; two at Church House Banbury in 1954 and 1955 and one at Wykham Hall on the Banbury Schools Campus in Ruskin Road, Banbury in 1957. A fourth was held at Wykham Hall in 1960. Each ran for three nights and were well supported and received by packed audiences.

Pete Shaw of 1st Bodicote in a sketch with a cub in the 1960 Gang Show.

A sketch by 2nd Banbury Cubs in the 1960 District Gang Show at Wykham Hall, Ruskin Road, Banbury.

Two photos of the opening ceremony of the Guild of Old Scouts annual Collaboree held in the Peoples Park, Banbury about 1959/60.

The left hand photograph shows on the left of the square 2nd Banbury led by Mrs Moore and Ron Vallender. Facing the the Officials, 7th Banbury led by Reg Thomas and Eileen Dean. The right hand photograph shows the the remainder of 7th Banbury and the right hand side of the square shows 1st Bodicote led by Ted Davidson and Cliff Wightman and 1st Ruscote led by John Pyne and May Baddeley.

The gentlemen with their backs to the camera are from left to right; Norman Blinkhorn, Superintendent Buckingham (Banbury Police Station) Bert Golding (District Commissioner) and Bob Green and at the bottom right-hand corner Bill Gibbs and Charlie Herbert.

A competition based on Scoutcraft was organised by the local branch of the Guild of Old Scouts in 1953 (an organisation set up nationally for former members of the Movement which was extremely active locally). The competition was named "The Colaboree" and was held in the Peoples Park, Banbury usually in the spring of each year, although initially in September. It took the form of a series of activities for Cubs based in the park and a series of tasks for Scouts based in and around the town centre. The event was very popular and ran for several years.

Two events were also organised for Cubs, one was a Cub sports day and the other was a Cub competition involving a series of tasks held within a local hall based on the Cub training programme.

Other events continued to be held including the Scout District Flag Camping Competition and the Annual joint St George's Day Parade with the Girl Guides.

The St Georges Day parade became one of the highlights of the year with Scouts and Cubs, Guides and Brownies parading to a different church each year headed by marching bands until it became too large and had to be held in St Mary's Parish Church as it was the only one large enough to hold all of those on parade. I recall the parade service having been held in St Mary's, Marlborough Road Methodist Church, Christ Church in Broad Street, Grimsbury Methodist

2nd Banbury's Rover Crew and guests following an investiture of new Rover Scouts in the chapel in Broughton Castle in 1952/53. Back row (from left to right) Tom Pratt, Candy Chandler, Harold Hobbs, John Pyne, David Partridge, Colin Wain. Centre row (from left to right) Cliff Wightman, J R "Tec" Railton (District Commissioner), Geoff Powell, Front row (from left to right) Gerald Foreshew, Norman Humphris, Ron Vallender, "Vic" Parry.

Church in West Street and on one occasion in Sibford Gower Parish Church.

Sometime in the early 1960s I was asked to be the parade marshal for the parade, a task that involved all aspects from assembly to dismissal and included the organisation of the colour parties in the church. My first parade was in St Mary's Church and, as was the practice, a rehearsal for colour parties was held in the church on the preceding Friday evening. During the course of the evening I approached a small group of Guide leaders who were talking together. Included in the group was a lady named Miss Biddy Wakelin. Biddy was the matriarch of Guiding locally who had run most successfully since 1933 the 1st Grimsbury Girl Guide Company. Biddy was a large lady and had always reminded me of one of the ladies in a McGill seaside postcard although when you got to know her, or rather when she got to know you, she was a very pleasant lady. As I approached the group Biddy saw me and I said to her "Could you please tell me your parade order" to which she enquired "Who are you?" to which I replied, my chest swelling with pride "I am the parade marshal" She replied, her chest swelling with indignation " Not of my parade you are not!" I retreated speedily. It would seem that there was some unwritten understanding that the two parades were quite separate and it was purely coincidence that the two parades started at the same time, attended the same church, had the same service and dismissed at the same place. It was just that no-one thought to tell me. In later years relations did improve considerably between the two movements. In retrospect it would seem that the animosity of the 1920s between the two movements locally lasted for many years and did not end until the early 1960s.

An event organised by Scout Headquarters in about 1950 was the National Bob-a-Job week held during Easter school holidays which was enthusiastically taken up locally and in 1954 £135 was earned by Scouts and Cubs in the District. This national event had its origins in 1944 when Scouts were asked to find some kind of a job on Saturday 20th May 1944. The money earned was used to fund the work of the Scout War Relief teams that were being set up to work in liberated Europe. Bob-a-Job Week continued for many years being renamed Scout Job week on the decimalisation of our currency and only ceased when it became politically "incorrect" to ask young cubs and scouts to call on people that they did not know seeking "work".

I recall as a young scout doing Bob-a-Job week; it was great fun, though the scheme was open to abuse by the general public, for example asking a scout to do two or three hours work in return of a bob (5p). I never experienced anything like that although I do recall a friend of mine in the 2nd Banbury Troop, Danny Jordan complaining one week that he had been asked by a near neighbour in Albert Street to help her on washday by turning the handle of a big, heavy clothes mangle. This he did for virtually all of the morning and at the end of the time the neighbour said "here is a thrupenny bit (just over 1p) only I'm hard up this week".

CHAPTER ELEVEN

Building a Solid Base

The 1960s saw a further expansion of the Movement and also an increase in the number of activities organised at District level. A Scout Group was started at the Ruscote Methodist Church by John Pyne a former Cubmaster at 2nd Banbury and towards the end of the decade a Group was started in Mollington by Frank Wroe, who had been a Scout Leader in 1st Bodicote, which went under the title of North Banbury. Although the Group was based in Mollington there were satellite branches set up in nearby Cropredy, Warmington and Shotteswell. A Scout Group was also started at the Friend's School in Sibford and 1st Adderbury was reformed by the vicar of Adderbury the Rev Vivian.

On the down side the three school groups closed, they were 3rd Banbury, 2nd Bloxham and 2nd Sibford.

The late 1950s early 1960s saw two Groups acquire their own head-quarters; 7th Banbury built a freehold purpose built headquarters in School Lane, Banbury which was opened by Lord Saye and Sele in March 1962. 1st Bodicote acquired a second hand wooden building which had formerly been a works canteen at the aluminium works in Southam Road, Banbury which they transported and rebuilt as their headquarters on the Kings Field, Bodicote. This was formally opened in March 1960 by Lieut. Gen. Sir Edward Grassett.

Before he started North Banbury Scout Group Frank Wroe had been a very capable and inspirational Scoutmaster and Rover Scout Leader with 1st Bodicote where he was instrumental in organising a number of events for the Group. One of the first was a competition, which was open to any Scout Troop nationwide, named the "Big Hunt Game" this involved a series of tasks which had to be carried out within the Troop's local area followed by a weekend camp in Bodicote. This met with con-siderable success. Not to be outdone in 1965 some of the Leaders at 2nd Banbury (who enjoyed the friendly rivalry between the two Groups)

Lieut Gen. Sir Edward Grassett inspects the Scouts at the opening of 1st Bodicote's new headquarters on Kings Field, Bodicote in March 1960, escorted by the Group Scoutmaster, Ted Davidson. Photo courtesy of the "Four Shires" magazine.

organised "The Banbury Cross Walk" which involved all of the Groups in the District combining together (something that had never been done before) with representatives from each Group walking in teams of two in hourly relays for 48 hours around a circuit which included Banbury Cross, Bodicote Scout Headquarters and Broughton village, with the aim of seeing how far they could cover in the time. At the end of the time they had covered a total of 223 ¼ miles. This spurred Frank and his crew into fresh activity and in 1965 a four man team entered the "Four Inns Walk" in Derbyshire – Frank ended up unexpectedly in the team after Robin Bygrave (who later became the first of only two organising secretaries of the Tour de Trigs) injured his leg whilst skiing in Kandersteg. The scratch team failed to finish the hike retiring at the Snake Inn (!!) but found the event a positive experience. Out of this experience Frank's Rover Crew discussed the possibility of organising something similar locally but as the local area was "too flat" every hill would have to be tackled –the "Tour de Trigs" was born! – A fifty mile night hike to be completed within twenty four hours. The first "Tour" took place on 31st April/1st May 1966. From small beginnings this event has now grown into one of the best known competition hikes in the country and as I write it is now in its 42nd year. It is the only national event organised by Scouting in Oxfordshire and one of the few organised nationally.

In 1967 the whole of the Scout Movement was revamped with a change of name, a change of uniform and many other administrative changes. The word "boy" was dropped for our title; Boy Scouts became Scouts, Wolf Cubs became Cub Scouts, Senior Scouts became Venture Scouts and Rover Scouts vanished entirely from the scene. The scout uniform underwent a dramatic change; out went the big hat in came the beret, out went the shorts and in came long trousers, out went the short sleeved shirt and in came the long sleeved shirt. The training programmes for all sections were completely revamped. Adults were no longer referred to as Masters or Mistresses but as leaders; Scoutmasters became Scout Leaders and Cub Mistresses became Cub Scout Leaders. The structure of a Scout Group did not change nor did we lose our scarf or neckerchief and the cubs retained their cap.

Following the retirement of Bert Golding as District Commissioner a newcomer to the District, Ron Beck became DC for a short while before handing over to Harold Hobbs. Harold did a marvellous job of welding the District together and it was during his time that the District began to take off. He oversaw the implementation of the new uniforms and the new training programmes and also set in motion efforts to establish a new District Headquarters.

In October 1968 the local Round Table agreed to raise funds for a new headquarters. A large sponsored walk was organised starting and finishing at Banbury town hall following a route that took in a number of villages; in total a distance of twenty miles. Over 340 people took part and raised £1,790. A site for a new headquarters was found in Duke Street, Grimsbury and negotiations began to turn this idea into reality.

I took over from Harold in May 1969 and one of my first tasks was to look at the viability of the headquarters project. It soon became clear that it was a non starter and so I approached the Round Table and asked if the

money could be used for the acquisition of a camp site which after dis-
cussion they agreed to. A site was found at Horley on an eleven acre field
owned by Trinity College. A twenty year lease was entered into and by
investing the money raised from the sponsored walk the income more
than paid for the rent. The camp site has proved to be a most successful
venture and now not only provides local Scouting with its own camping
and activity centre but produces income which helps run the District.

CHAPTER TWELVE

A Second Golden Era

The period from 1970 until 1985 was the second of the District's golden eras. During that time the number of Groups increased significantly and the number and variety activities organised at District level also increased. The whole District was moving forward at a considerable speed.

With regard to Groups in the District, 1st Grimsbury and 5th Banbury (St Johns) who were on the point of collapse were reinvigorated. 1st Banbury was restarted and after a short while, due to its success-ful growth, was divided into two separate Groups; 4th Banbury (St Paul's) operating out of St Paul's Church hall in the Warwick Road and 6th Banbury (St Hugh's) operating out of St Hugh's Church hall in Ruskin Road, Easington. Over the next few years more new Groups were started in town; 8th Banbury (Bretch Hill) in the Church hall in Prescott Avenue, Bretch Hill, 9th Banbury (United Reformed) in the United Reformed Church hall, by Banbury Cross, 10th Banbury on the Hardwick estate, Banbury and 11th Banbury on Cherwell Heights estate, Banbury.

In the villages two groups, 1st Deddington and 1st Adderbury were on the verge of closing and they were reinvigorated. New Groups were formed (or reformed) in Hook Norton, Bloxham, Hornton and Sibford. By January 1986 there were 18 active Groups, including a District Venture Scout and Ranger Guide Unit, in the District with a membership in excess of 1,000.

More Groups acquired their own premises, 1st Grimsbury in East Street, Grimsbury, 4th Banbury in the old mission hall at the junction of Warwick Road and Neithrop Avenue and 6th Banbury on Banbury School Campus in Ruskin Road, Easington.

The District opened its own "Scout Shop" supplying uniforms, books and equipment to members and Groups which was run by volunteers, ably managed for over 30 years by my wife, Janet. It was run initially

At the District's Annual General Meeting held in the Great Hall at Broughton Castle in 1976, Ron Marchington (2nd Banbury and Ethel Isham (4th Banbury) were each presented the Scout Association's Medal of Merit. An award that they richly deserved. The photograph was taken following the presentation of their awards. From left to right. Ron Marchington (2nd Banbury) Ted Hayden, (Scout Association headquarters staff and secretary of the Scout Association) Trevor Parry, District Commissioner. Peter Rowland Jones (Deputy County Commissioner for Oxfordshire), Ethel Isham, (4th Banbury).

from our home but following the opening of 6th Banbury's headquarters it moved into one of its rooms from which it still operates.

A District Scout band was formed which ran successfully for many years and which included Guides within its membership.

The District's finances were put on a sound financial footing thanks to three District Sponsored Walks, where the proceeds were divided between the Groups and the District, together with funds generated by the District Scout Shop and the District Camp Site.

The number of activities organised by the District increased greatly. The District agreed to take over the running of the Tour de Trigs Walking competition from 1st Bodicote as it was putting enormous strain on the Group's resources. District Cub and Scout Swimming Galas were held at the outdoor pool in Park Road, Banbury. District Cub and Scout Fishing Competitions were held on the Oxford canal adjoining the Southam Road, District Cub and Scout Sports were held on the playing fields at Banbury School, Ruskin Road. District Scout Camps (to replace the District Flag Camping Competition) and District Cub Camps were held at the Horley campsite.

The District also organised a series of footballing activities. These were efficiently run by Ken Broome, a parent of two Scouts in 2nd Banbury. There was a District Scout Football league and a District Cub Football league during the winter months. The winners were presented with their trophies and medals at the Spencer Football Stadium (home of Banbury United) where they played a representative XI made up of players from the other teams taking part in the league. At the end of the season an indoor five a side football competition for both Cubs and Scouts was held at Spiceball Leisure Centre, Banbury. These were remarkable for their split second timing that enabled the event to run literally like clockwork. There was also a summer competition held on a local football ground usually in one of the villages. Ken later became District badge secretary, (only the third such secretary since the 1930s) a position he still holds.

At national level the District was also successful; a Scout from North Banbury Group won his class on two occasions at the National Scout Sailing Regatta and Championships. Two Scouts from 1st Bodicote also performed well. In 1964 an Oxfordshire County Rally was held at Blenheim Park, Woodstock to "Meet the Chief Scout" One of the organised activities was "Scoutcar Racing" a formula for racing peddle cars (a sophisticated form of peddled soap box). Several District Groups entered and 1st Bodicote were successful in several races in their "Bodicar" which included components from a redundant trek cart and a steering wheel from an old Austin Seven car. From 1964 onwards several groups entered the National Scoutcar Races which were held at a different seaside venue each year; 1st Bodicote, 2nd Banbury and 1st Banbury (soon to become 6th Banbury) achieved considerable success, notably 1st Bodicote who were class winners on four occasions and collected some dozen or so podium finishes.

Bannesburie Venture Scout and Ranger Guide Unit were far from inactive and for a number of years organised expeditions into the mountains of Wales and the Lake District. In summer, they organised expeditions abroad (following the tradition of 3rd Banbury (County School) Troop) to places such as the Lofoten Islands, Norway, Iceland and Canada all ably led by Ron Sangster, a former member of 2nd Banbury.

In 1983 I resigned as District Commissioner to take up a position at County of Deputy County Commissioner for Oxfordshire. Ron Marchington who as a boy had been a scout with 1st Wardington Sea Scouts and as an adult, a leader (including many years as Group Scout Leader) with 2nd Banbury and for some time my Assistant District Commissioner for Adult Leader Training, took over as District Commissioner.

CHAPTER THIRTEEN

Unlucky for Some

Ron took over at a time of great activity and progress within the District. A new training section was introduced nationally; the Beaver Scout Section for boys aged six and seven. It was at this time that numbers in the District exceeded one thousand, making it the largest District in Oxfordshire. Ron did not have the best of beginnings as DC as shortly after his appointment he suffered a massive heart attack. However despite this he continued leading the District. From its peak in 1986 when there were 18 groups and 1,024 members in the District Scouting declined both nationally and locally. Slowly over the next few years Groups began to close or closed some of their training sections, i.e. a Beaver Colony, a Cub Pack or a Scout Troop. This was a situation that continued following Ron's retirement at the age of sixty five and it continued to dog the next three District Commissioners.

In 1990 girls were allowed to become Beavers, Cubs and Scouts although since 1967 girls had been allowed to become Venture Scouts.

I recall telling my troop of 27 Scouts at 2nd Banbury about this change by Scout Headquarters at a scout meeting the evening following the announcement. I asked the troop if they wanted girls to join their troop. The result was that a reluctant five scouts agreeing that they did. Whilst waiting for the troop's answer I overheard one scout mutter "but not my sister". So I rephrased the question. Did they want girls, excuding sisters, to join their troop? The response was an immediate and enthusiastic yes.

Girls now make up a small minority of the Movement's membership; about 5%.

Perhaps this book should be correctly titled "Scouting for *Banbury's* Boys and Girls".

Slowly bit by bit many of the activities organised by the District ceased to happen; the District Band closed following problems with its leaders with one faction leaving the movement to form the Royal British Legion

(Bodicote) Youth Band. This became a successful and prestigious band which is still going strong today. Even the successful football competitions folded until by January 2004 there were only 335 young people in the District; its lowest level since just after the second world war and lower than in the 1930s. However since 2004 there has been a steady increase in numbers, increasing to nearly five hundred young people in January 2008. Some activities are once more being organised at District level, for example District Cub and Scout Camps. Through all this period of decline there have been bright spots; The Tour de Trigs has continued to be organised and the District Camp site has been developed and expanded. The site now extends to over forty four acres of field and woodland and can now offer a wide range of activities to its users from rock climbing to archery.

CHAPTER FOURTEEN

In Conclusion

Henry Ford is reputed to have said that "history is bunk". I would dis-
agree quite strongly. History gives us a clue to what works and what does
not. Take Scouting locally for example. The District grew and was most
successful on three quite separate occasions thanks to the enthusiasm,
dedication and hard work of those at the top. Firstly in 1910 to 1913
Norman Braggins the District Scoutmaster and Syd Mawle the District
Chairman enabled scouting to grow from very small beginnings to a
viable and successful District. Secondly in the 1930s the remarkable
efforts of Geoffrey Fiennes (later Lord Saye and Sele) and his Assistant
District Commissioner, Tec Railton rescued Scouting locally from almost
certain oblivion to become a major force within North Oxfordshire and
thirdly in the 1970s and early 1980s the dedicated team that I gathered
around me of Ron Marchington, Eric Woodhouse, Ron Sangster, Maurice
Lane, and the late Ethel Isham and Bob Grainger saw the District grow to
its largest recorded membership and period of greatest activity.

The District was not successful in the 1920s when there appeared to
be a complete lack of leadership from the top to such a degree that at one
time there were, for a short while, no cubs or scouts in Banbury although
they existed in the villages around. A similar lack of effective leadership
also appears to have arisen in the last ten or so years, which is a great
pity. Baden-Powell once said that Scouting is a movement rather than an
organisation; movements move organisations do not. I think that in
recent years the District leadership has lost that willingness to move for-
wards rather than backwards. Fortunately things of late appear to be
improving driven by the grass roots of the movement; that is by the Scout
Groups themselves.

Scouting continues to play an important part in the provision of
quality training for the young people of North Oxfordshire thanks to a
small group of dedicated adults who understand and appreciate the

value of the Scout training programme in this modern world. Just over one hundred years since the founding of the world's greatest youth movement and one hundred years since it came to North Oxfordshire let us hope that locally it will soon enter upon its third golden era. It has waited long enough.

The B-P Guild of Old Scouts

The B-P Guild of Old Scouts was set up nationally to provide a social facility for former Scouts who did not have sufficient time to give to scouting on a regular basis but who wished to meet with other former scouts from time to time in a social setting and to help on an occasional basis scouting in their locality.

The Banbury branch of this national organisation was formed on 30th May 1949 and is the only section of Scouting in the District which has retained a full record of its activities in the form of a minute book and a cash book.

The committee of the Banbury branch, immediately following formation, set about organising a series of monthly meeting at which speakers were invited to attend to speak on a wide range of topics. It also organised an Annual Dinner.

In 1953 the branch organised a competition for Scouts and Cubs of the District which was held in the Peoples Park, the cubs remaining in the park whilst the scouts were set projects around town. The event was called the Collaboree and was a great success and continued for many years.

Also in 1953 the branch began assisting at the annual St George's Day parade and service acting as stewards and taking the collection.

The branch became a very important part of the District organisation and in many respects took on the role of the District Committee which at that time was not very active. Many of its members were in fact active Scouters which was not the original intention of the branch but was in fact the way that it developed.

This pattern of events continued for many years, however following the radical changes made to Scouting nationally by the Headquarters' "Advance Party Report" in 1967 and with the appointment of a new District Commissioner in 1969, who revived the District Committee, but

mainly due to the dwindling numbers and increasing age of its membership the branch closed on 31st March 1973.

At the final meeting at which the decision to close was taken the
minute records that the District Commissioner told the meeting that
"With the best of intentions he must criticize. He felt that the Guild had
not moved towards integration on becoming part of the Scout
Association, [one of the changes brought about in 1967] and tended to
carry on in the old way. The Guild was five years behind local Scouting".
He said "Scouters were really concerned for their boys which left little
room for the Guild and in his view this was how it should be. The Guild
would have to organise through lay members"

The loss of the Guild was sad but there is no doubt that in the years
that it was active it played an important and at times a critical role in the
wellbeing of scouting locally.

The following article appeared in the November and December 2005 issues of the "Four Shires" magazine and is reprinted below together with some additional text to bring it up to date.

The "Tour de Trigs" Walking Competition

Around this time of year – October, November, you will often see, at weekends, small groups of walkers making their way along some of the many footpaths and bridleways of Banburyshire. The chances are that they are practicing for the annual Tour de Trigs walking competition which takes place on the first weekend in December.

For those not familiar with the event it is a fifty mile competition hike, mainly at night, around North Oxfordshire and the surrounding counties for teams of three walking along a set route (given to them minutes before they start) visiting hill tops and using poorly defined footpaths and bridle ways, the aim being to complete the course as a team in less than twenty four hours.

The Tour has its origins in an event started by a group of Rover Scouts attached to the 1st Bodicote Scout Group way back in 1966. The young men having taken part in the Four Inns Walk in the Derbyshire Peak District the previous year decided that they would organise a similar event around Banbury. However to add a degree of difficulty to the walk they decided to make the walk a night hike and to add interest the route would take in as many Ordnance Survey Triangulation Points (Trig Points) as possible. Invariably trig points are situated on the tops of hills. (Or were; they are now rapidly becoming obsolete with the advent of Global Positioning Systems [GPS]). And for a name they chose a corruption of the famous cycle race the Tour de France and called it "The Tour de Trigs Walking Competition"; their enthusiasm being greater than their French grammar.

The first competition, which took place in May 1966, was a very low key affair with teams entering from Scout Groups around Banbury and slightly farther afield including Coventry (who produced the winning team); about eight or nine teams entered. The route, which had been previously announced well in advance, started from 1st Bodicote's headquarters in the village and went east over the River Cherwell and then northwards to Claydon and then via Edge Hill to Brailes and on to Cherrington, through Whichford and then via Sibford Gower , Swalcliffe, Shutford, and North Newington, over Crouch Hill and back to Bodicote.

I remember well taking part in that first competition; it was a warm, sunny spring day and there was a very relaxed atmosphere about the whole event. Teams of three set out at two minute intervals and soon everyone was on their way. We visited check points along the route and had our cards marked to show that we had visited the checkpoint and were invited to have a cold drink which was very welcome. As day turned to night the going got harder and by the time my team reached the spinney on top of Brailes Hill (Highwall Spinney) I was ready to retire. I had been walking with a thumb stick (similar to the walking sticks now used by mountain walkers and the like) and unfortunately I had developed a blister between my thumb and index finger and one of the marshals had very kindly given me a plaster. (Later I was to learn that when my retirement was reported back to hike control in Bodicote the marshal stated that one of the walkers was retiring with a blister on his thumb to which came the reply "Bloody hell is he crawling!") It took quite while for us to get off Brailes Hill as the person responsible for picking up retirees had gone to a dance and we had to wait for him to return home.

The following year the event was planned to take place again in May but due to a very low number of entries the event was postponed until November. But it was not to be as the area was by that time suffering from an outbreak of foot and mouth disease. The event was therefore cancelled and organised again for the following November. (The Tour in 2001 was also cancelled because of foot and mouth disease.)

In 1968 I again entered the Tour with two colleagues Ron Sangster and Brian Tucker. This time about twenty teams entered from around Banbury and further afield. We were fortunate enough to win the competition, in I think, just over sixteen hours - quite a reasonable time.

One of the problems besetting the organisers in its early years was getting sufficient support staff to man all of the check points with the result that some teams of marshals had to man, in succession, a series of check points which meant that if the front runners were making good time and the back markers were going slow then it was very difficult for the marshals to be in place when the first team arrived. This happened to us when we won the event. Arriving at the check point at Sibford Elm crossroads towards the end of the walk and way after midnight we arrived at the checkpoint at the same time as the marshals and as a result we had to wait for them to set up and get us a hot drink. In view of the delay we asked for a time credit which was refused on the grounds that we shouldn't have been going so fast!

A similar occurrence happened a few years later when I was chairman of the organising committee.

That particular year a team of Wembley Sea Cadets entered the hike. They were soon setting a cracking pace and it became increasingly difficult to get check points opened in time to greet them. By the time they got to Brailes Hill (Highwall Spinney) in the early hours of the morning they were really putting the organisation under pressure and they arrived at the check point at the same time as the marshals. As the marshals dumped their kit one of the walkers spotted a plastic bottle and exclaimed "Ah water" grabbed the bottle, unscrewed the lid and put it to his mouth. A horrified marshal saw what was happening and shouted out "No, it's paraffin" and at the same time knocked the bottle out of the walkers hands. But not before the walker had got some liquid into his mouth. The marshals demanded that the walker retire but he would not hear of it and insisted on continuing, which he did. He did however retire at the next check point. What had happened on Brailes Hill was reported to me back in hike control. I was also told that the walker had retired at the next check point. I then asked "Was he ill?" to which the response came "No he ran out of paraffin". The walker was in fact unwell and was taken to The Horton Hospital where he was detained for a day or so with burns to his lungs.

If I had been that young man I would not have wanted any more to do with the walk ever again, but the following year he turned up with his team mates determined to win. Yet again they set a cracking pace and managed to get beyond Brailes Hill without incident. But as the team were in sight of the check point at Margetts Hill (just to the north of Long Compton Woods) the young man collapsed face downwards into a large muddy puddle. His team mates picked him up and carried him in a semi-unconscious state to a caravan which was serving as a check point.

Whilst all this was happening hike control had asked me if I could go out to the Margetts Hill check point as radio contact had been lost, to see what the problem was and to do whatever was necessary to rectify matters. This rather concerned me as responsible for the check point was a young employee of mine, Michael Vincent whom I had persuaded to help on the hike (I like to think he volunteered). As I approached the check point in my new car and totally unaware of what had been happening at the check point I was greeted with the sight of

Michael, outside of the caravan waving me down. (My first thoughts were "I know it's late and I know he and his team are lonely but as a greeting that's a bit over the top".) I drew up alongside him and wound the window down to be greeted with the words "Oh Mr Parry I think we've killed someone". I jumped out of the car and rushed into the caravan to see a body laid out on one of the beds. It appeared to be breathing but very shallowly. I then enquired what had been happening and was told that the walker had been dragged into the caravan by his two team mates and had been laid on the bed but every so often he would come too and shout "Mother", get up and dash out of the caravan and run down the road only to collapse again and have to be dragged back to the caravan.

Having taken stock of the situation I decided that the only thing to do, having no contact with the outside world, was to put the walker into the back of my car and get him to hospital as quickly as possible, which, with the help of his colleagues is what we did. (Have you ever tried putting an unconscious, dirty body into the back of a new car? It's difficult and leaves the interior of the car in quite a mess). After a quick dash and further alarms the young man was ultimately delivered to the Horton Hospital - yet again - where he was detained for a further couple of days before being released.

The next year the team entered again but without the young man who had caused so much trouble on the two previous walks. On enquiry I was told that he was not entering because he had joined the Royal Marines!

Nowadays this kind of problem is unlikely to arise as there are now medical checks carried out by a resident doctor prior to walkers commencing the hike and throughout the hike there are mobile rescue teams stationed around the course. These are supported by a mobile field ambulance service and first aid facilities back at hike control.

In order to be able win one of the many trophies that are on offer a team has to be able to do two things; they have to be able, as a team, to walk fifty miles (not as easy as it seems with a failure rate of over 60% most years) and be able to read a map. Failure to read a map correctly can have disastrous consequences. Several years ago one team managed to walk off the edge of the map –and they ended up in a police cell!

The first hike control knew of their misfortune was when a call was received from the Shipston on Stour Police Station asking if we had lost three walkers. We then asked for their team number which the police gave us and we were able to confirm that they were in fact participants in the hike. We were then asked to send transport for them as currently they were residing in the police cells, which of course we did.

It is not only walkers who cause problems, sometimes it is the marshals.

One year during the height of the IRA bombing campaign of mainland UK the route took the walkers past Compton Wynyates House and a checkpoint was set up on the adjoining Windmill Hill. One member the marshalling team was a young man who was a new recruit to the event. During the course of the evening it was realised that water was getting low and the new recruit volunteered to walk back to Compton Wynyates car park (now closed) to collect more water from the reserves held there. This is where his problems started. Having climbed to the top of Windmill Hill in daylight he was now trying to descend in total darkness. He soon became lost and a journey which should have taken him no more than 45 minutes there and back took him almost three hours. On his eventual return he told, but only when asked, that very soon after leaving the check point he had got lost and tried to retrace his footsteps, but without success and after wandering around for some considerable time, climbing hedges and jumping ditches he saw a large house with a light coming from a downstairs window. He made for the light and ultimately knocked on the adjoining

TOUR DE TRIGS   95

door. The door was answered by a man. The marshal told him he was lost and asked where he was and how did he get back to Windmill Hill. The man it transpired was the Duke of Northampton. His Grace then proceeded to tear a strip off the marshal for disturbing him in the middle of the night. After all, the marshal could have been the IRA. The marshal then said that the Duke told him "where to go" in no uncertain terms.

The Tour de Trigs has always been supported by Scouting not only in Banbury but also in Oxfordshire. The whole event has been organised since its inception by Banbury Scouts. One year whilst chairman of the organising committee I was asked by the County Commissioner for Scouts in Oxfordshire, Paul Gore (Paul was, before he retired, a career civil servant having been Deputy Governor of the Gambia for many years) if he could attend the walk and could bring with him Lord Baden -Powell the grandson of the founder of the Movement, Robert Baden-Powell (B-P).Of course I said yes.

On the day of the hike notices were put up around the hike headquarters advising that Lord Baden-Powell would be attending at some time during the hike. Most people thought that it was a joke.

Lord Baden-Powell (who was staying with his aunt and uncle in Wigginton) duly arrived with the County Commissioner and after talking with the headquarters staff asked if I would take them out onto the hike route. Having visited the check point on the top of Brailes Hill we then called in at the checkpoint at Sibford Elm crossroads. By this time it was around two in the morning. The check point was in a caravan. After talking to the staff inside we stepped outside where we were met by about three teams all arriving at once. Turning to them I said "May I introduce you to Lord Baden-Powell" I immediately realised that this was a mistake. The look on the faces of the walkers seemed to say "Look mate we've just walked over 35 miles, it's dark, it's cold,

we're hungry and we're tired and we've still got 15 miles to go and if you think that we are amused think again" –or words to that effect. Before any of the walkers could reply Lord Baden-Powell stepped forward saying "I really am Lord Baden-Powell" There then followed a very amicable conversation followed by requests for his Lordship's autograph which he willingly gave.

On the way back to hike headquarters my two guests suggested that next year we should enter as a team. Some team; a lord of the realm, a deputy colonial governor and me! – I declined; discretion being the better part of valour.

One of the major problems for a competition of this nature is communications and for many years this consisted of field radios supplied and operated by the Sea Cadets and by the use of public phones. One year we experimented with some TA mobile equipment but it was not a success, for example at a check point near Farnborough the radio operator was having difficulty receiving any signals and after trying manfully for a very long time exclaimed "I can hear them". To which one of the marshals replied "And so you should I can see them (the mobile unit) just down the road. End of experiment.

The advent of mobile phones has of course made communications so much easier but it has also brought its problems. A few years ago a team phoned in to the hike control to say that it was retiring and could they be picked up in about an hour's time and gave a map reference. The person in hike control became suspicious as he could hear music in the background and on checking the reference discovered that it was that of a public house. The call was not treated as urgent.

It's not only during the hike that problems can arise but also sometimes afterwards. At the close of the hike there is always lunch followed by a presentation of trophies and certificates and it is always the tradition to invite the Town Mayor of Banbury to attend the lunch and to make the presentations afterwards. Miss Florence Woollams was the first Town Mayor following local government reorganisation and she had the unenviable task of setting the standard for future Town Mayors and an excellent job she made of it too. It therefore followed that she should be invited to the closing ceremony of the tour. It was my job as chairman of the organising committee to chair the proceedings and to host the Town Mayor. After a very long stint that had started before dawn on the previous day and had gone on through the night and into the following day, by the time it got to the presentations I was feeling a little bit tired. However I stuck to my task as best I could. During the introduction to the presentations it was my custom to give few statistics about the hike; how many had entered, how many had started, how many had finished and the like. As an introduction I said to the large assembled audience of walkers, marshals, staff, friends and relatives that although so many had entered quite a few had not turned up on the day. "Clearly the event", I said, "was quite a daunting challenge and the excuses for not taking part were many and various. For example one person had said that he was in bed with flu" to which I added the remark that "I thought he said Flo". I thought no more about it and continued through the rest of the ceremony to the end. After the Town Mayor had left one of my colleagues came up to me and said "What on earth were you thinking about when you made the comment about flu and Flo" to which I replied I didn't understand what he was getting at. To which he said "What is the first name of the Town Mayor?" "Florence" I said and "What is the diminutive of Florence" he continued. To which I almost replied Flo and then I realised what I had said. Fortunately the Town Mayor was not upset. Unfortunately it is now too late for me to apologise in person.

It is quite often only after the hike that walkers experience "problems" particularly in respect of sore feet and even worse. I remember several years ago seeing a young lady in the early hours of a Sunday morning walking, boots in hand, across Blessed George Napier's assembly hall. What attracted my attention was the fact that she seemed to be wearing one white sock and one red sock. Then to my horror I noticed that whenever she put down her red sock it left behind an imprint in blood. I am sure there are many similar untold tales of pain and suffering after every hike.

The hike despite its occasional problems continues to be a great success and to be run with a remarkable degree of efficiency and it now attracts entries from all around the globe. So what started as a small local affair is now international and an established part of the long distance walking calendar. This is thanks to a loyal and hard working group of people and to the continuing support of many competitors and the help and co-operation of local farmers and landowners, all of whom share the enthusiasm of that small group of Rover Scouts all those years ago.

One of those many hard working people is Ron Sangster who not only walked in the first hike and was part of the team that won the second but has for over twenty five years been organising secretary and hike controller of the Tour de Trigs. It is due in no small measure to his unstinting hard work on behalf of the hike that it has continued so successfully all of these years. It was therefore fitting that at the end of the 2006 hike (His twenty fifth hike as organising secretary and hike controller.) he was presented with a special trophy as a mark of appreciation by his colleagues; much to his surprise and the delight of the assembled audience.